# COSMIC PROFIT

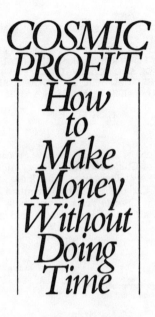

# COSMIC PROFIT

## How to Make Money Without Doing Time

Raymond Mungo

*An*
*Atlantic Monthly Press Book*
Little, Brown and Company      Boston/Toronto

FIRST EDITION

Portions of Chapter Two have appeared
in *California Living;* of Chapter Three in *Rocky Mountain Magazine;* of
Chapter Four in *New Roots.* Lines from "The Choice," from *The Collected
Poems of W. B. Yeats,* Copyright 1933 by Macmillan Publishing Co., Inc.,
renewed 1961 by Bertha Georgie Yeats. Reprinted by permission of M. B.
Yeats, Miss Anne Yeats and the Macmillan Co. of London & Basingstoke
and New York.

*Library of Congress Cataloging in Publication Data*

Mungo, Raymond, 1946-
  Cosmic profit.

  "An Atlantic Monthly Press book."
  1. Small business—United States—Case studies.
2. Subculture. 3. Mungo, Raymond, 1946-
4. Businessmen—United States—Biography.
I. Title.
HD2346.U5M86    650'.12    79–26366
ISBN 0–316–58933–0

ATLANTIC–LITTLE, BROWN BOOKS
ARE PUBLISHED BY
LITTLE, BROWN AND COMPANY
IN ASSOCIATION WITH
THE ATLANTIC MONTHLY PRESS

Designed by Janis Capone

*Published simultaneously in Canada
by Little, Brown & Company (Canada) Limited*

*PRINTED IN THE UNITED STATES OF AMERICA*

*For Bob Kaplan,*
*counselor extraordinary*

# Acknowledgments

Many people helped me to write this book, not the least of whom were the managers and employees of nearly all the businesses I visited. They are too numerous to mention here, but I do appreciate their cooperation and support. For particular and invaluable help at various stages of the project, I am eternally grateful to: *Seattle:* Peter Miller, Cathy Rogers, Judy Thompson, Tom Robbins, the mad deacon, the Freedmans, Dan Levant, Alan Furst, and Brook and Sarah Stanford; *California:* Cynthia Williams, Don Doner, Bruno from Coast Business Machines in Monterey, Paddy Grinstein, Tom Farber, Amanda Spake, and Vida Blue; *New York:* John Wilton, Raphael Clark, Sara Bershtel, Brian Kellman, and David Beach; *Boston:* Eric Utne, Peggy Taylor, Sandy MacDonald, and, of course, my parents and family; *New Orleans:* Steve and Judy Diamond. A special thanks to my editor, Peter Davison, and to the Carmel Institute for the fellowship which enabled me to complete this book.

*"Money is a kind of poetry."*
—Wallace Stevens

# Author's
# Note

To begin with, Wallace Stevens sold insurance. He also wrote some good poetry. Those of us who never bought insurance from him may remember only the poems, but certainly there are beneficiaries (or their heirs) of his policies who never read his work but appreciate his insurance. Dick Gregory said, "Insurance is like *me* betting *them* that I'm gonna lose!" Personally, I've taken out insurance only when required to do so by banks or agencies which mortgaged my homes or financed my automobiles; neither my health nor my life has ever been insured, though both have been jeopardized from time to time. I am afraid that if I actually paid money to insure them, I would have to have accidents, get sick, or even die to make back my investment.

Now I have invested a fair amount of time, energy, and money in books. It's a question of priorities. My own sense of security is heightened by having plenty of volumes of my favorite poets, and no insurance policies, hanging around the house. To each his own.

But this is not a book about insurance. It's a book about business, and I bring up Wallace Stevens at the outset only to make the point that business and money

are topics of such infinite personality and com-
plexity — even spirituality — that it's difficult to judge
other people's business objectively. In the course of
researching this book I spent weeks with tycoons of all
sorts and as often as not ended up realizing that I had
only the beginnings of notions of what truly motivated
them. In some cases it was the pure love of money —
"the root of all evil" — but money itself is superficial
and boring. Yet I've never met a person, including the
most exalted religious leaders, who was indifferent to
its power. We are all in business and money is our
common denominator, our mutual passion.

Initially, I searched for a new kind of business, a
business of new ideas, the apparently instant successes
we've all read about and dreamed of for ourselves. The
better mousetrap. The marketplace is rife with products that we consumers never could have imagined a
few years ago. There's big money in natural foods,
natural soaps, weird footwear, metaphysical notions,
new games, vaguely psychological self-help methods,
quasi-Eastern religions, paramedical aids, "communal" and "collective" corporations, new magazines
and newspapers catering to special interests that
scarcely existed before, recreational equipment, arts
and crafts, cottage industries, and many more.

Behind every one of these new businesses is a person
or group who jumped into a fresh idea and created a
demand. But tastes change faster than presses can roll,
and at this moment — any moment — new products
are becoming passé and even newer notions being
born. So we don't want to make the mistake of taking

the products themselves too seriously. They will all turn to dust, and generally faster than anticipated. It's the people who create the business and their attitudes toward their work which interested me. The "labor force" fills jobs but each of us dreams of being his or her own employer. We naturally want to own our time, our own lives. At our worst we imagine that mundane profit, plain cash, can make it possible.

But all of the old clichés about money are undoubtedly still true. Cash doesn't seem to guarantee anybody a satisfied mind or any free time. There *must* be, I thought, there *ought* to be, a different kind of profit, the kind that gives people a way to make a living doing what they enjoy, enables them to live free in their hearts. It is the rarest kind of profit, the gift of life, energy runaround, cosmic profit — the sense of being restored and excited and energized, rather than drained, by a day's work.

We can hope at least that Wallace Stevens enjoyed selling insurance. It's hardly outside the capacity of our imaginations. We all sell something, so we might as well be proud of it. This book won't teach you all the mechanics of going into business for yourself, but it does tell tales about some people who did it with varying degrees of success. Your business will be as personal as the inside of your skin, as unique as fingerprints. Nobody can tell you how to do it, and there is no guaranteed formula for success.

When I was in my twenties and burning through the 1960s as if there'd be no tomorrow, *work* was an odious term to me. I wanted to play all day, to live for free. But we're into the 1980s and I'm into my middle thirties and *work* has become a beautiful word and the best possible "play." Work is life. It is its own reward, and when it's good we know it, we're happy, we're onto cosmic profit.

(Don't forget to take it easy, though. Anything you chase after will run away.)

# COSMIC PROFIT

# 1
# Time
# Is
# Money

*"The real cycle you're working on is a
cycle called 'yourself.'"*
— Robert M. Pirsig

My son was born just two months before we opened
our first bookstore. It was 1973 in Seattle, and I had
previously had no interest in children *or* business but
suddenly found myself passionately involved with
both. Marriage and children will put the fear of God
into any young man; it seems one is not *allowed* to be
broke anymore. Ironically, we didn't make any money
to speak of in the first couple of years of our bookselling careers, but I consoled myself with the thought
that my son would see his father not as the employee
of a real estate agency, a job I'd held for all of four
weeks, but as a self-employed writer and businessman.
That self-employment also allowed me plenty of time
to enjoy being with him in his infancy, and although
we were so poor we had to eat dinner out on credit
cards we never paid for, at least the kids had free access
to every children's book in print.

I went into business with two partners, Peter Miller
and Judy Thompson. We were all twenty-seven years
old and shared a profound distaste for commerce and a

great love of good books. It rained almost every day in Seattle that year. The unemployment rate was staggering and thousands of homes in the city had been abandoned by mortgagees who couldn't make their payments. It did seem the wrong time to be settling in Seattle and the worst imaginable time to go into business there. Our friends thought we were crazy, but actually the bookstore was an effort to *keep* us from going crazy. There were no "good" jobs around and even the "bad" jobs were unavailable to us because we were "too educated."

Peter Miller, following Harvard and the founding of a storefront school in Roxbury, Massachusetts, was taking odd carpentry jobs and restoring blown-out old Seattle houses. Judy Thompson was reduced to tending bar at a funky place called the Gaslight on Capitol Hill. (It's gone now, replaced by a *soissant* restaurant with pseudomedieval motif.) (*Soissant* means chic.) I watched even large royalty checks disappear into the yawning jaws of "the cost of living"; it got so bad that I ended by calling up landlords from the back room of a highly unethical real estate rental agency.

The agency, like others of its kind, existed on the basis of stealing money from people who were desperate to find rental housing in the city. Despite the economic crisis in the area, which left houses for sale at bargain-basement prices on every block, houses for *rent* were more scarce than ever. The new listings published daily in the Seattle newspapers were few and were invariably taken within twenty-four hours — sometimes within minutes of the papers' hitting the streets. The agency threw up an office in an empty storefront overnight and within a week was advertising in the "For Rent" columns of the newspapers a dazzling array of houses and apartments at astonishingly low prices.

The beleagured home-searcher, reading these ads, called the phone number given and got a fast-talking salesman who promised the moon. The client had to pay $25 (nowadays these outfits charge $50 or more), for which he or she was entitled to inspect its "exclusive listings" daily, with the generous time limit of a year. They "guaranteed" you would find a home.

Thousands of people fell for it, and still do, although this particular agency is long gone. There never were any "exclusive listings," of course. That was where I came in. As the lowest-paid employee and the only one who did not sell the service directly to the customer or realize any commission on the sales, I simply provided the listings. I had to get each day's newspapers as soon as they came out, and also every weekly or community newspaper I could find. Then I'd call the landlords at all the new listings, referring to the previous day's or week's edition to weed out the repeat ads, and ask their permission to place their listing at no cost to themselves. About half of them consented. The others hung up or berated me. I have never attempted to defend the agency — "Lookit, mister, I don't own this place and this is just a job to me, and you know how hard it is to get a job in Seattle?" — but it was exhausting work to have strangers screaming at me on the phone all day.

The point is that by the time my listings were typed up and handed out to the poor souls milling about in the store lobby, they had already appeared hours earlier in ten-cent newspapers, and if the rental was desirable, *it was already taken.* I never met a person who actually found a home through the agency. The surprising thing was that the great majority of its customers never realized that they were being taken; or, if they did, never mentioned it. Every day a few hysterical customers — driven to the limits of their patience in chasing down apartments and houses that had long since been rented — would be led into the manager's office to be denied their refunds. The manager was always armed, as protection against rival rental-agency hoods.

The few weeks I spent in the back room at the agency seems in retrospect a kind of personal hell through which I deliberately put myself in order to come out the other end chastened enough to do *anything* to preserve my time for myself. If time is money, and your time is your own, you are certifiably wealthy. My separation was painless: I simply called in from the hospital where my son was sleeping and informed my armed employer that I had to stay home now and take care of the baby.

Five months later, the agency disappeared, leaving its employees owed several weeks' back pay and its customers in the lurch. Operations of its kind still exist in some United States cities. They are perfect examples to us that crime does pay if you're mean and stupid enough to victimize other people who trust you. The owners were paranoid, competitive, apparently miserable. They lived in hotel rooms out of suitcases, had no friends or families. They paid for their misdeeds in the extreme poverty of their lives. They were the kind of guys who spend Christmas Day in a barroom. And they proved that some people try to get rich selling absolutely nothing at all.

Now, our bookstore wasn't trying to get rich. Our loftiest goal at first was to be able to make a hundred bucks a week for each of three people. In those days, a hundred a week was plenty to live the high life in Seattle. We planned to stock only books which we admired or at least respected — no Hallmark cards, junk fiction, "stationery supplies," novelties, posters, bumper stickers, or any of the other sidelines that some bookstores carry. We called the place Montana Books because we had some dream about retiring to a ranch in Montana when our ship came in.

We hired an artist to create a logo based on a specific mountain in Livingston, Montana, one which the local people claim has the face of Christ in its ridges. The artist, Norman Skougstad, painted our shop windows and fled to Africa, where he became an expert on Ouagadougou, Upper Volta. Our first window-washer scraped half of his paint job off by accident and we left the window half-painted because Norman alone could have restored it. It made the shop look old even when it was brand-new. We took our motto from Henry James: "One should never be both corrupt and dreary."

We chose an abandoned storefront on a block with no prospects. It was within walking distance of our houses, which had no prospects either. The store had been used as a real estate agency, insurance office, novelty-printing firm, and attorney's office, all businesses that had gone under at that address. No retail experience. The neighboring greasy-spoon café had been closed down by the city for health violations. Next came a stereo shop that went bankrupt. Then a corner laundromat. But fortunately there was one popular business on the block: the United States post office. And people had to pass our bookstore to mail their letters.

We went to work cleaning out the crap left behind by all the businesses that preceded us, saving useful items like file folders, rubber-stamp ink pads, and receipt books. The place looked like the aftermath of a bombing. Our hearts sagged under the burden of making it presentable — making it beautiful. At the very bottom of the rubble we found an old wooden shingle with the name of Seattle's then-mayor, Wes Uhlman, on it. He'd started his law practice there.

A crew of fourteen or fifteen volunteers swarmed over the store. They built a balcony of stained hardwoods — and wooden shelves, tall and short; a sales booth. Sawdust was everywhere, and everything was behind schedule. On the night before we opened, not one book was yet on the shelves. We spent the last week working through the nights. The books were placed on their shelves — covers facing forward to fill up the awesomely empty spaces — after dawn on the morning we opened, Dec. 8, 1973. The first book we sold was *Winnie the Pooh*.

Montana Books, Inc., was floated on $5,000 and undetermined amounts of credit from major East

Coast publishers. The five grand came from the neighborhood bank, the Pacific National or "Pacific Irrational" in our private moments, which loaned it to us based on collateral of some shares in I.B.M. which had a market value at the time of $9,000. You could say the Pacific Irrational was not exactly extending any trust in us, but you could hardly blame them. No serious observer believed that we could survive. Peter Miller's father owned the I.B.M. shares and loaned them to us. When the market faltered in 1974 and the shares dropped temporarily to a value less than what we owed, the bank immediately demanded a cash payment to offset even the slightest possibility of losing money on us. Peter Miller told the sixty-year-old female chief officer of the bank, "Sam" Coleman, that I.B.M. would still be in business when her bank and all its branches went under. Sam was a direct and forceful character, and shortly thereafter came steaming into the bookstore hollering, "All right, Mungo, hand over the credit card!" (It was overdrawn.)

We changed banks after the loan was paid. In fact, we've changed banks every eighteen months or so since we started. Never did find a bank that would put up with us for long. We never owe money to the banks when we leave 'em — in fact, owing money means you can't leave 'em — but neither is there any love lost. In recent months I've been titillating a Japanese bank (Seattle office) with the notion that it should invest in us. The tellers don't speak English, which can only work to our advantage, and the funds are channeled through Tokyo, which would give one's check some time to clear. I was raised with a working-class vision

of banks as tyrannical foreclosers of people's mort-
gages, an attitude that was nurtured in my parents'
generation by the grim Depression years. Movies and
television taught me that bank-robbing is heroic
activity. If I find myself, in adult life, still profoundly
antagonistic toward financial institutions, I'm at least
being consistent.

As for the credit from major publishers, it's only fair
to admit that many of them had no idea how much
credit we would take if given the chance. I sat down
and wrote the most seductive letter I could honestly
sign, printed up hundreds of them, and sent them to
every large publisher in the United States, with
individually typed salutations and envelopes and individual signatures. The letter announced that our corporation would open the store shortly, and requested
a current catalogue, a visit from the publisher's representative in the Northwest, and an open-account
basis of doing business: "30 Days Net." I listed the full
names and home addresses of the owners; the name of
our bank, branch, and personal banker — the afore-
mentioned Sam — such few credit references as we
had; and I'm sure I mentioned that our line of credit
was based on I.B.M. shares without specifying the
number of shares or explaining the fact that they were
locked up in Sam's vault.

It worked surprisingly well. Some publishers are
professionally cautious and sent us complicated credit
application forms, which I dutifully filled out. Some
extended us limited credit on a kind of trial basis, but
the limits were as generous as $1,000 per account. And
some even extended us an apparent carte blanche! We

filled the empty spaces on the shelves by simply ordering the books we needed without regard to our utter inability to pay the bills on time. Within six months, the store was becoming well stocked and the collection agents were calling us from 10 A.M., opening time, until 2 P.M., which is really 5 P.M. in New York, daily. A collection agency in New Jersey, which seems to specialize in dunning booksellers on behalf of publishers, habitually called Peter Miller's home number when he entered his office at 9 A.M. Jersey time . . . pre-dawn in Seattle.

"Mr. Miller, Mr. X here."

"Mr. X? What time is it?"

"Nine o'clock."

"Where are you calling to?"

"Washington. You're in Washington, right?"

(We later *hired* Mr. X to dun those bookstores who never paid us for the books we publish and distribute, which shows you how tables turn. All our bills got paid eventually, of course, or Montana Books would have long since disappeared; and today we have a stable enough clientele to keep current on bills. I can't particularly recommend the way we got started in business, but it was the only way open to us and we always believed we'd make it, even when nobody else did.)

The idea of being "in business" was unattractive to the point of almost being immoral. This prejudice, which resembled in a crazy way the British aristocracy's disdain for "tradesmen," was a legacy of the mad 1960s, when we'd turned against "the establishment," which included the government, the universities, the churches, *and* Capitalism. I was buried in Milton, Donne, Shakespeare, and Keats rather than Marx or Engels, and I didn't even know precisely what "capitalism" means, but I knew I was against it. Capitalism to me was simply business. Business was simply money. And money was the one thing in this world that drives everybody crazy.

But the idea of cash flowing through our hands, even if much more was owed out than coming in, was one we felt perfectly comfortable with. The shopkeeping part was tedious, especially in the first year, when customers were few and you could spend a whole afternoon without seeing a soul or getting a phone call. I read many more invoices, packing slips, catalogues, and discount schedules than novels by Faulkner or poems by Yeats. We patiently assembled our own collection of favored books and writers, but were driven by boredom or ambition (who knows the difference?) to organize readings, lectures, performances, and demonstrations and to begin publishing and distributing books to other bookstores. We speculated (correctly) that we could perhaps sell more books out the back door (which faced on the post office's delivery entrance) than over the sales counter.

While looking for land in the hills around Seattle, my wife and I met a pleasant, late-middle-aged woman named Gen MacManiman, who, with her husband, Bob, had lived on the same small farm in Fall City for more than thirty years. Bob was a trained engineer who had abandoned his daily commuting to the Boeing Company to work full-time on their cottage industry, a sturdy wooden food-dehydrator. Gen got interested in food-drying years earlier when she was drying herbs she had gathered from the countryside for medicinal purposes. They developed their Living Foods Dehydrator through many levels of improvement over the years, and manufactured a really efficient, enormous dryer for about $80 retail.

But in 1973, when we met them, the MacManimans had sold fewer than five hundred dryers, and the business provided only a secondary income. Gen's principal energy was still going into her role as an herbalist and lecturer on natural health and natural foods; Bob still took engineering assignments. Gen also operated a mail-order book business specializing in health, nutrition, and religion. "The general idea," she said, "is to piece together enough of a living to let us stay home and do what we *like* to do." And she smiled her warm, real smile — the kind of smile that lights up a room. The MacManimans lived modestly in a two-bedroom farmhouse but obviously made the best and most use of all the resources of the land, and their kitchen was always overflowing with great smells, their hearth crackling with gnarled eucalyptus, neatly split alder. They were "poor" people who seemed rich.

Toward the end of our visit, Gen showed me a little yellow pamphlet she had written in response to customers who bought the dehydrator and "are always pestering me for a recipe book to use with it." It was called *Dry It You'll Like It* and had a very amateurish appearance, printed on heavy stock and held together with staples. But it also had an irresistible charm. It was not typeset but hand-lettered in a fine calligraphic script, had cartoon illustrations and a bright canary-yellow cover. Gen had printed a thousand copies of the book and hoped she could sell all of them within two years, mostly to people who bought the dehydrators. She had included in the book the blueprints and instructions for building a Living Foods Dehydrator at home, reasoning, as she said, that "anybody who would take the extra time and trouble to build their own dehydrator would use it well."

My commercial antennae began vibrating. It was a time when corporations pandering to fear of famine in the general public were offering "family survival kits" of dehydrated food for outlandishly high prices. Food-drying was definitely something that the natural-food freaks could get into as a sweeping national fashion, I thought. *Dry It You'll Like It* was the first book I'd seen which catered specifically to home food-drying and told you how to do it yourself. There were recipes for drying meat, fish, bananas, tomatoes, apples, fruit leathers, even honey and peanut butter cookies for grandchildren. I told Gen she'd better get ready to print a hundred thousand copies, and she laughed. And laughed.

Montana Books became Gen's distributor. And *Dry It You'll Like It* has sold over a hundred forty thousand copies in its first four years as a glossier, perfect-bound trade paperback at $3.95. Thousands of those were sold one copy at a time out of Gen's living room directly to readers who had heard about it by word of mouth. The book was advertised once in *Organic Gardening* and in a few other, more esoteric, publications. We first peddled it only to other bookstores in Seattle; I'd actually drive over to the University (of Washington)

Bookstore in my red 1954 Mercury to deliver five copies of *Dry It*. The book sold well from the first, and rumors flew around. Soon other stores wrote to us asking for it. And not long after that we were selling three copies of *Dry It* for every one copy of any other book in the store.

So we invited Gen to give a food-drying demonstration in the store, and billed her with a Bellevue, Washington, chiropractor, Carl Jelstrup, who was famous in the area for New Age health techniques. The idea was to have an evening of natural-health and natural-food ideas, although the three proprietors of Montana Books were all smokers, drinkers, and eaters of anything that came along. For that matter, we didn't *read* the many health and nutrition titles that we became well-known for selling, but our single copy of the *Complete Poems of Wallace Stevens* had been on the shelf for a year and, as I've said, the collection agents were hot and heavy on our case. We were, as a business, showing the good sense to survive and already our high literary and moral ideals were undergoing some corruption.

Hundreds of people packed the store on the night of Gen's and Carl Jelstrup's demonstrations. Jelstrup called for a volunteer from the audience to help him prove that sugar was detrimental to our bodies. The woman who came forward was asked to lie on her back on a massage table. Carl placed a sugar cube on her chest, in the cleft of her breasts actually, then ordered her to "resist!" as he yanked her arm downward from its upraised position. Then he removed the sugar cube, raised her arm, ordered her to "resist!" again, and *voilà!* could not budge the arm more than an inch. The crowd loved it. He did it over and over with different volunteers. Then Gen came on with the dried-food demonstration, and had brought enough dried fruit with her to feed the entire audience. Everybody munched pear leathers and dried apricots while she showed how to use the Living Foods Dehydrator. The balcony shook so much from applause we were afraid it was going to fall down. One time the vibrations of our show-business success were so strong they blew out the front windowpane, leaving Virginia Woolf and Emma Goldman exposed to the rain.

Meanwhile, back at the farm, Gen and Bob had stepped up production on the dehydrators to the point of having five full-time employees making them — still in wood and still by hand. The cartons of *Dry It* had taken over the living room, where shipping-room help was hired. A new room was put on the house just to keep the *Dry It*s warm and dry. The MacManimans' sudden good fortune was eaten away in large part by the I.R.S., as Gen and Bob had never previously made enough money to develop sophisticated tax planning. Other books with home-drying chapters and whole books about drying appeared, and *many* kinds of dehydrators cropped up in health-food stores. The frantic pace of business slacked off some, and sales of the book and the box leveled out at a more comfortable rhythm. Gen had an automobile accident, which forced her to slow down for a while. Bob died of natural ailments from which he'd been suffering some years. When I last saw Gen, in 1978, she was looking relaxed and well, had "come through" her success as basically the same warm person I'd met five years earlier, and was talking of a revised edition of *Dry It* with new recipes.

As a postscript to the story of Gen MacManiman and *Dry It*, I should add that she was approached by several major publishers with offers to buy the rights to *Dry It* and pay her a royalty on every copy sold, but she turned them down. Gen's point of view was that it would be foolish to take a 7 to 10 percent publisher's royalty when she could realize 30 percent of the value of each book by publishing it herself. Which is interesting when you consider how many people publish their own books in the hope that they'll come to the attention of a major house. But *Dry It* is one of those rare books that sell themselves to an audience which is eager for the information. And the major publishers invariably wanted to replace the calligraphy with typography, or reduce the page size, or do something else which would destroy the "home-made" quality of the book in Gen's view. In her case, I'm sure she made the wise decision in keeping her home industry at home.

Montana Books was only a step away from home. It was so quiet there on a normal day that I could have my infant son sleeping in an improvised nursery in the back room. But *Dry It You'll Like It had* put us in the wholesale book business, and that seemed to be our best hope of paying the monstrous bills the bookstore had accumulated. Even the great success of Gen's effort hadn't given us more than enough to eat, as every dollar that came in was greeted by a green ogre demanding two. We looked around for another book that we could publish or distribute.

I was at that time talked into the idea that the Bates Method of vision exercises could salvage my failing eyesight. The method was created by a Dr. W. H. Bates of New York at the turn of the century and was so popular and respectable in the 1940s that the U.S. Armed Forces used it to try to help men excluded from service for vision problems. Aldous Huxley met Mrs. Margaret Corbett, Dr. Bates's chief disciple, in L.A. and claimed that the method had spared him from becoming permanently blind. He wrote a "little book," *The Art of Seeing*, in gratitude to Mrs. Corbett and Dr. Bates, in which he described the Bates Method's approach to common vision defects. The exercises are simple enough, things like sunning and "palming" the eyes, "swinging" one's gaze in a pendulum-like arc back and forth around the room, *practicing* "the art of seeing." But the science of ophthalmology is complex and subtle, and Huxley warned the reader to use the book in conjunction with the services of a profession- ally authorized Bates Method teacher. I went to "see" Elin Gilbert, an astonishing old lady who'd been giving Bates lessons from her downtown studio for more than twenty-five years. She was a former ballerina and Montessori educator, twice-married, who seemed to know more about vision than anybody in the world. She was so relaxed she could fall asleep in the middle of a sentence, and relaxation is one of the big factors in the Bates exercises. The premise is that the mind affects vision, so that even damaged or imperfect eyes can be improved by psychological or mental means. By the time I'd spent an hour with Elin, I'd go wandering off dreaming of her childhood in Norway or the green fields of Vermont and actually *think* I could see. I even drove my car without glasses for a time.

But I couldn't find a copy of Huxley's *Art of Seeing* anywhere. Published in 1942 in London and New York, it had been quite successful but had been out of print in the United States since the early 1960s. The British edition, not generally available here, is one of a multivolume set of Huxley's work and as such is set in small type. The used-book stores in Seattle knew the book but said that they sold every copy they got hold of. One store had several people waiting for a copy.

It seemed inconceivable that a book by Aldous Huxley could be out of print and still in demand. It was, furthermore, improbable that Huxley's publisher, Harper and Row, would be willing to surrender the rights for the small kind of advance that a tiny Seattle company could offer. But the only expense in proceeding with what I sensed could be a commercial success was the cost of a phone call to New York City. I put off making the call for a week. But Harper and Row, as it turned out, was willing to sell us the United States paperback rights for an advance of $500. I borrowed the $500 from Gen MacManiman.

We had the book entirely reset in a larger typeface and paid a local artist to design a simple red cover illustrated with Judy Thompson's eyeball. We also added a new preface, which Laura Huxley, the author's widow, graciously provided, and a couple of photos of the Bates exercises in use. We did all of this, as we had started the business, with absolutely no clear idea of how we were going to pay for it. The typesetting and first printing of 10,000 paperback copies cost slightly more than $10,000 and our final check to the printer (for $3,000) bounced, bounced, and bounced a third time before he (the printer) lost his mind and tried to seize the books, of which we'd already presold 4,800 copies on credit. In fact, Montana Books automatically extended credit to bookstores because we had no mechanism with which to gauge their creditworthiness, and couldn't very well be pious and sanctimonious about it when we were so much in debt to the publishers ourselves.

Three years later, we've sold between 35,000 and 40,000 copies at $4.95 — hardly the giddy success of a *Dry It You'll Like It,* but enough of a success to belie Harper and Row's conviction that the book had no market. But I was too lazy to keep up with my own Bates exercises, and today wear glasses just as before, if a somewhat reduced prescription. And I ended up with an addressograph machine and thousands of mailing plates under my personal custodianship. It was almost a throwback to the sixties, with its mimeo machines and radical-politics offices. I felt too *old* to be standing there all afternoon shooting envelopes through the machine.

The last few weeks of production work on the *The Art of Seeing* were insane. We were always at the press, working on our orders and the mailing labels so as to be able to ship the books out as soon as they came off the offset, working on publicity in our half-conscious way, mailing out flyers to prospective bookstores, health groups, even optometrical associations, which were sure to be hostile to the Bates approach. We dug up addresses for all the eye doctors' colleges. And libraries, which, we reasoned, might well have tattered old copies of the book, much read by the patrons, and need replacement copies. And Bates teachers and pseudo-Bates teachers from the new generation of believers. We never felt we had enough money to advertise, and to this day the book has never been advertised but was reviewed here and there. Like *Dry It*, it sells by word of mouth, to readers who are themselves trying to correct vision problems.

During the last few days at the press and bindery, none of us slept at all. I worked through the night and all day long for three days and nights, and then collapsed on the sidewalk in front of the Lincoln Pharmacy, across the street from Montana Books, just after the last of the books was delivered. A couple of guys in their twenties came to my rescue, picked me up and helped me across the street to the bookstore, which was closed for the evening. As I splashed water on my face and tried to compose myself, the rescuers were eagerly examining the thousands of copies of *The Art of Seeing*, which were piled up in cartons every-where. They wanted to buy a copy right then and there and I should have given them one in thanks for their help. But my mind was so clouded with exhaustion and confusion that the idea of selling a book made me want to burst into tears. I pleaded with them to come back in the morning and buy a copy from the clerk. I knew I wasn't capable of writing out the sales receipt and making change. But they were eager for the book, and insisted. And so the first copy was sold after-hours in the darkened bookstore by a near-comatose clerk. Fortunately, they had the right change. I was left standing there surrounded by mountains of Aldous Huxley, gazing dumbly off into space, with $4.95 cupped in my palm.

In 1975 we incorporated the publishing and distributing company into a separate corporation with the same owners at the same address. Montana Books, Publishers, Inc., lived in the glassed-in office in the back balcony of the store. Its stock was right on hand, as one large room functioned as warehouse, shipping room, and editorial offices. Every afternoon found me stuffing Zippy bags with *Dry It You'll Like It*, *The Art of Seeing*, and increasing numbers of other titles: rural skills books from Cloudburst Press in Canada, which is run by a delight fully intense young entrepreneur, Vic Marks, who lives in the woods with a telephone and I.B.M. typewriters but no indoor toilet; naturopathic and homeopathic tomes; remaindered copies of my own and my friends' books (it takes some of the pain out of being remaindered if you can get your hands on the books — even Thoreau supposedly insulated his walls with unsold copies of *Walden*); assorted magazines; poetry. We distributed anything we liked, and sent out flyers to our burgeoning mailing list, and sent bills, which were often not paid for a long time if ever and were called the Accounts Receivable. I took the goddamn Accounts Receivable home with me, if not literally, at least in my heart. I went to bed at night wondering if the Anytown Bookshoppe was ever going to send in its $67.82. The publishing company at this stage took in more money than the bookstore company and had to cover the bookstore's obligations. But as they were separate companies, the publisher had to officially *loan* its money to the bookstore. It was weird; we were loaning money to ourselves but the two companies had come to have identities of their own — as if they were people distinct from us. And from each other.

Something had to change. I stopped long enough to remember myself as an idealistic youth. Could I have imagined then that I would even *know about* Accounts Receivable? Some lucky customer was sitting in the balcony in a canvas rocker reading a novel while I was trying desperately to finish *Publishers Weekly* before a new issue arrived. We stood all day packing books for shipment in our amateurish Zippy bags and handwritten addressing, lugged the packages up and down stairs, kept logs and records of books and money coming and going, got *more* desperate the more successful and serious the business became, found ourselves being *owed* $50,000, spent more as more came in and still didn't have any left over, and still had new bills from printers and binders and dozens of utilities and services, including grand sums dropped at the post office. We got more and more angry at the Anytown Bookshoppes of the world, which were using our little balsa-wood ship to float their own yachts. And in 1976 we went to a cash-only policy.

Most publishers, including us, give bookstores a 35 to 40 percent discount on the retail price of the books. We raised the discount to a scale between 45 and 55 percent and agreed to pay all shipping costs ourselves — but we demanded a check with every order. Other bookpeople in the Seattle area warned us that it would cut into our sales considerably if we denied reasonable credit, especially to stores whose creditworthiness was beyond reproach. But we felt we couldn't discriminate in this policy — we knew that once we started trying to figure out who to trust, we'd go crazy very quickly. So we denied credit even to B. Dalton and Waldenbooks, whose checks are issued by a computer with nearly-perfect reliability. We had to write soothing letters to many good customers explaining that we were not contesting their creditworthiness, but merely Lacked the Facilities for billing. And this move did cut into our sales, of course, but we were more than happy with it — actually ecstatic. Every book we shipped was paid for. No returns. We never had to send bills to anybody. The Accounts Receivable trickled in for a year or more, then the hopelessly uncollectable ones were written off. I went to sleep peacefully at night again.

The business of publishing is a bit like babysitting, except the babies in this case are the books. You have to keep them somewhere warm and dry and send them out in well-packed, careful parcels. It had long seemed to us that these custodial functions could be organized around a warehouse, which would service as many as a dozen small presses in the city with one shipping system. We finally got the warehouse in 1978, a funky old warhorse of a building on the waterfront, by the city's Public Market. Madrona Publishers of Seattle rented it and took Montana and Cloudburst and a

bunch of other small publishers under its wing as our
distributor. We all rode around on dirty trucks hauling
tons of cartons of books from every back-room store-
room the small publishers had been using. I told
myself that Hell must be having to walk around with a
sixty-five-pound box of books. But the mighty effort
paid off as our books got a full-time babysitter in
Madrona Publishers, and we were left with nothing to
do but come up with editorial inspirations. We have
only one customer, Madrona, which sells our titles,
takes its cut, and pays us the rest. Bookstores can get
the books on credit again, but Madrona takes the risk.
Now at the time this transition took place, Madrona
consisted of only one man, Dan Levant, who had
heretofore worked out of his home office, which was
adjacent to his living room, which was gradually filling
up with books. He'd been warehousing Madrona's
titles elsewhere but was forced to move them, and
Peter Miller talked him into the Warehouse Scheme.
Less than a year later, Dan's got about five or six
employees and the warehouse is buzzing along. Montana Books, Publishers, is a "phantom company." It
exists, but all its people are gone. Manuscripts from
hopeful authors still come in, and people write nice
letters thanking us for the Huxley. I even got to dance
the diddly-bump with Laura Huxley in Aldous's ala-
baster living room. The publishing company brought
us wonderful times and fortunate introductions, a
certain business acumen achieved of massive pain and
struggle, and now a quiet resignation. It floats along in
limbo, but every now and again it mutters to be reborn.
I try to ignore its protests, because I know that *that*

way lies frustration and grief. But as I survey the cypress trees of Monterey, California, I can't help worrying about Dan Levant.

Every year's business at Montana Books has been better than the year before, but we recognized a real, finite limit to the amount of business we could do in one small store somewhat off the beaten track. Aided by our readings, parties, and seminars, we'd become widely known in the city, and the store eventually went to being open nights and then Sundays. Now, it's closed only on "real" holidays like Christmas and Thanksgiving. While it will never make us rich, it did withstand the traumas of its first three years and survived in the face of what seemed overwhelming odds against it. There were many moments when we wept over ledger books and considered "blowing it up." The thousands of unpaid-for books weighed on our backs and minds and life was grim, tedious, profitless, and discouraging. By 1977, however, we were in our fourth year and the store had at last turned its corner. It could support a few clerks and pay its bills; it kept its customers and acquired more; and it was boring as hell. Judy Thompson moved back to Minneapolis. Peter and I moped around looking for something to do. The idle mind is the devil's playground, and next we found ourselves thinking that we were ready to go downtown and create a new bookstore that would generate some "serious money." Play with the big kids downtown, blow them away, that kind of pride-before-the-fall. I was also going through a melodramatic divorce and as a newly single man had many lonely hours to fill up. Peter, too, had recently taken to solo quarters. We had to find enough work to drive us to distraction from our miseries.

The Seattle *Weekly* had moved out of its storefront offices in Pioneer Square, the oldest part of Seattle's downtown waterfront — a neighborhood that includes derelicts and drunken Indians and gospel missions as well as chic boutiques and first-class restaurants. One of those restoration projects many U.S. cities now have to preserve the Old World charm of "historic" red-brick buildings at up-to-date prices. A natural scene for the tourists in the summertime. The *Weekly*'s storefront was in the old Saint Charles Hotel building, which had once been the city's poshest whorehouse. The newspaper moved upstairs to more commodious offices, and we of course plunged into the lease on the store.

And we did the whole crazy thing again. The crew, the sawdust, the balcony, shelves, and a mountain of books. All this, as Peter pointed out, just to have a place of our own to hang out in Pioneer Square. We borrowed $20,000 from the bank across the street and $5,000 from a customer. We called the place Miller & Mungo Booksellers, since Thompson appeared to be permanently in Minneapolis, but Miller & Mungo was owned by Montana Books. And Miller & Mungo stocked all 3,000 Dover titles and specialized in books on building, architecture, graphics, engineering. A craftsman's bookstore. Not one novel or volume of poems. Pottery, silversmithing, yes; Tolstoy, no. Giftie things like Tutankhamun for the tourists. It was and is a more sophisticated evolution of our original store, which by now has taken on most of the qualities of a church. You lower your voice and take off your hat when you go in there.

And Miller & Mungo, like Montana Books before it, had to go through a long first year with very few customers and mounting debts to publishers, anxiety, hostility, and worry. It *was* easier the second time around. And we did throw an opening party at which we served vodka punch to about five hundred people, some of whom then danced in the streets of Seattle. And held readings, hung out, and met a whole class of Seattle downtown types who would never have made it to our establishment in the Wallingford district. We ran an ad for the new store every week in the *Weekly* with a different quotation or remark each time — things like "Sex without love is better than love without sex" (Jack Spicer) or Peter Miller's recipe for "Jewish water": it was tap water in a Tropicana orange juice bottle left in the fridge for two or three days. (Even though Peter's Jewish and made up the joke while I was down in San Francisco running a booth at the Book Fair, *I* ended up having to placate the picketers from B'nai B'rith.) We got behind on our payments to the bank across the street and I started entering the Saint Charles Hotel from the alleyway door in the hope that the mastodon of a proper banker would not detect me from his office window. The profits from Montana Books and Publishers were nothing compared to the staggering losses at Miller & Mungo Booksellers and we'd managed, *somehow*, to come through four years of successful business, have two stores, a publishing company, a warehouse, a dozen employees — and *still* not have enough money between the two of us to buy a drink in the corner saloon. It was depressing.

I fled the city in 1977, for the better part of a year. I placed one of those "writer needs quiet country house in which to work on book" ads and rented a posh vacation home in the mountains for nominal rent. It was at Index, Washington, a fishing hideaway on the Skykomish River with a village of 176 persons, a tavern, general store and post office, and an old inn. The Index Tavern was the real center of the community, the place where gossip is exchanged, beer is drunk by the barrel, where you go to find the handyman or the sheriff. It had a pool table, a T.V. with bad reception, a jukebox and pinball machine, and a country and western band on Saturday nights, when it spilled over in riotous celebration. Index was only sixty miles from Seattle but felt like the wilds of Wyoming.

Woody and Snooks owned the tavern. They kept a whole bunch of kids and grandkids in the back room, which led into their house. Woody complained about business all the time, said he was going broke except for the big holiday weekends, when hunters and fishermen up from the city jammed in the place and drank oceans of beer and ate whole microwave-oven pizzas. Some people in Index sat in the Tavern most all day. It was *lost* in there. But the brew is not my own ticket to Paradise.

Lucy, the postmistress, raised the American flag in front of the general store every morning. A brass postbox with a combination lock cost $2 a year. Barbara and Dottie, who have managed the store for a couple of years now, came down from Alaska, where they were both teachers, and shared a house. They were two vital middle-aged ladies from the north country, and Barb and Dottie revitalized the Index Store, which had been in a kind of perpetual gloom. They sold spools of thread and batteries, newspapers and frozen ground beef, groceries, beers and wines with an indomitable cheerfulness in the face of the town's poverty and idleness. Business improved.

The Bush House Inn served real cocktails, not just beer and wine, and full dinners, but it was not much patronized by the townsfolk themselves. It was "for the tourists." A second Woody and his wife Maureen run the place and are always talking about selling it. Woody's a retired Marine officer and also mayor of Index; Maureen writes patriotic poetry published in *Leatherneck*, the magazine of the Marines.

I lived about a quarter of a mile upriver from the blue iron bridge where these businesses met to form the town center, and walked into town every day for mail and gossip. But after some peaceful months in isolation, broken by occasional visits to Seattle and chores for Montana Books, I found that the woods became an unneeded insulation from the world. When I found myself driving to Seattle virtually every day to tend the bookstores and other business, I realized my great effort to recapture the bucolic myth was only a temporary relief. As much as my business drove me crazy, it was *my* business and could no more be ignored than my children. Even with a staff grown to fifteen or more people, it is a family kind of business.

In mid-1978 we finally couldn't take the poverty anymore. We opened a third store inside the Seattle city aquarium and sold film, postcards, T-shirts, earrings, and key chains to tourists. King Tut was in town, and about a million visitors came to our city. Aquarium patrons were made to go *through* the bookstore in leaving the facility, and, unlike our first two efforts, this store did bang-up business from its first day. We sold high-quality books about marine life and oceanography and serious stuff like that, but naturally most of the business was in nonbook items. The increased revenue from the aquarium eased some of the debts of Miller & Mungo, just as our publishers once covered the debts of Montana Books. Then the tourists went away on Labor Day and everything returned to normal.

But what is normal now for Montana Books is too serious for me. Somehow, try as we did to fail — guilty as we were about profiting — we managed to create a successful business, and now it rolls along like a giant machine. The paperwork is mountainous. My taxes, insurance, and debts are made more complex by my interest in this empire of printed objects. A bookkeeper, lawyer, and accountant have to keep track of it all. And I'm a mostly absentee owner.

Who knows where the energy for business comes

from? When I was feeling good and ready to consider deals of whatever magnitude, Montana Books was the perfect stage for my act. But too much exposure — even to the limited degree of a far, nice town like Seattle — makes a person feel put upon, burned out, tired. We found that we passed through cycles of interest in the business, ranging from irrepressible excitement to complete alienation. It became essential to remind ourselves that our presence was not required daily — that the institution we'd created *would* lumber forward of its own accord whether or not we were there. It's impossible to spend every day in a bookstore without going into an introverted or melancholic state. Some people really carry business to the level of being one of the arts of life. Somehow, I won't. But even the small extent to which I've engaged in it opened my mind to a new understanding, the corporate view. I learned there's nothing to success but unlimited amounts of hard work, and a little bit of inspiration.

Montana Books did not begin providing us and our clerks with a living wage until its fourth year, so we had to dabble in other businesses as well to generate enough income to stay alive. By far the most profitable one was real estate, as it's still the most inflation-prone and corrupt industry of all. It was an era of empty houses in Seattle, a time when you could buy a fundamentally sound house for under $20,000 with no down payment and easy terms. We scooped them up, and moved from one to the next after painting, wallpapering, sanding, scraping, staining, and selling at a profit. There's scarcely a house in the city, no matter how shabby, worth less than $60,000 today, and by the time you read this it might be a million.

I also parlayed an impressive stack of credit cards and bank loans into a massive personal debt that led me to a state quivering on the edge of bankruptcy. It all started with one little credit card in 1973. It was unsolicited. I had been living in Vermont since 1968, owned a hundred-acre farm, paid all my bills, and owed nothing. Every year, the local bank in our small town sent me a Bank Americard, which I returned with a letter saying I didn't need one. I believed, then and now, that credit cards are a major conspiracy by the banks to get us all in debt over our heads. Despite my protests, though, some computer continued to send me a card every year.

The day finally came that I needed it. I was traveling with my future wife in Costa Rica; she was pregnant and suffering a hip dislocation. With her two-year-old daughter, we were staying in hotels in San José and trying in vain to find medical or chiropractic help. Nothing worked. We knew we could have Jelstrup work on her hip if we could get to Seattle.

I swallowed my pride and asked the Vermont bank to reinstate the last credit card I had returned. It complied cheerfully, and the very day the card arrived in San José we used it to buy three one-way tickets to Seattle and to borrow about $100 in cash. We'd charged up $400 altogether on the card on its first day, and its credit limit was $350. Nobody in San José, Costa Rica, cared about its credit limit. And I wasn't worried because, after all, $400 was not such a staggering amount of money to owe, and I knew the bank would ask for only 10 percent of the balance per month — at 18 percent annual interest. Forty dollars owed next month, I figured. No cause for alarm.

But we'd arrived in Seattle with only $80, were staying with friends at first, and needed some time and money to relocate ourselves. Not to mention a doctor to work on my friend's hip and another one to deliver the baby. I found that keeping in touch with my editors and selling my writing was more difficult from the remoteness of the Northwest. Many evenings came when we faced the alternative of going hungry at home or dining out in style on our credit card. While hunger may be tolerable to adults, it is definitely not so to children, and we did the sensible thing. We ate, I signed, everybody nodded and smiled. And the bill mounted.

I then realized that the bill was getting sizable and the monthly payments more difficult. We were way over the limit and, unless some miraculous royalty check appeared, we'd soon be unable to make the payments. What to do? The solution was all around me in T.V. ads, newspapers, the advice of bankers: get more, and different, credit cards; don't use one up indiscriminately but spread your use around and develop reasonably good credit. Soon I was applying for more and more credit and getting it with a smile. Despite my indebtedness to Bank Americard, my "credit profile" was good: I owned some real estate and had a visible income — however unstable — from writing, was over twenty-five, married, had children, and had Montana Books.

Credit cards poured in. When I was in debt to one company the next company did not seem to care. I was building a reputation for myself as a "slow payer" in the closely guarded files of the local credit bureau in Seattle. There is a credit bureau in your town, or somewhere near it. But the ruination of my financial well-being happened slowly, over five years, and the credit bureau did not have all the information about what I owed, and it *did* list debts that were already paid. Until some more sinister computerized operation comes along, I think it's fair to say that most credit bureaus have very sloppy records, and the right hand seldom knows what the left is doing. I wound up with all the bank cards, all the oil-company cards, discount-store accounts — all the way up to the "prestige" cards like American Express, which sometimes have no firm credit limit. And for a long time — for years, while the game of juggling income to pay out checks in little envelopes with windows grew merrier — I actually believed that I could pay the bills. My little ship of state floated along.

But I didn't have great powers of self-discipline. More than that: when a friend desperately needed air fare to some distant point like Boston or Tahiti, I bought his or her ticket with nothing but my "good name." My wife and I took an all-expense-paid honeymoon. We were winners of a pay-later vacation most Americans dream of but wouldn't dare take, even when all the banks and credit companies virtually create the scenario in our minds. "Have a good time!" they shout. "Relax and don't worry about the cost!"

When the high life ended, the crash was abrupt. One

day a man in a business suit came to the door and asked if I was myself. I cheerfully admitted it and he demanded my credit card. Soon came the man serving court papers: sued for the first time at the age of thirty. That was before I knew enough to find out who's calling before admitting I'm in. If they can't get you on the phone, they can't get you. Armies of collection agents, swarming the earth like locusts, heartless and determined, they advanced on me. But my loss of credit and return to the cash standard also renewed my innate sense of priorities in life: food first, of course, then shelter and clothing. I no longer take these "big three" for granted, if I ever did. I stopped having a personal bank account two years ago and am living in a kind of bankless bliss. I am never tempted to write a check. I cash the checks I get either at the bank where they were issued or through a friend's bank account. All of my friends have bank accounts. I either have cash or I don't, but I certainly have no credit. I've wined and dined and played the big man, but if I'm somewhat chastened now, I'm also having a better time. I figure all my debts will get paid eventually if I don't run up any new ones. In this country, you're more successful the more money you owe, but the toll it took on my stomach linings was unendurable.

At this writing I'm a nomad. My business hums in my absence while I go up and down the West Coast in my company-owned Fiat. I learned the lessons of "company-owned" things ten years ago, when I bought and maintained a farm in southern Vermont for a communal, utopian group of artists and writers. Over four long Vermont winters, I had little else to do but study law books and corporation charters, and I created a company called Monteverdi Artists Collaborative Inc., to which I deeded my farm for $1. MAC, Inc., included as its trustees all the people who lived on our farm, and its stated "educational" purposes included writing, staging theatre and music events, publishing literary magazines, supporting artists through grants. Because it is organized as a nonprofit company, it cannot sell the farm to the profit of any individual(s); it now actually stages the Shakespeare that we merely dreamed about at the time we got our tax-exempt status from the I.R.S. Nonprofit is a good way to go.

I sat up nights on the farm and read government regulations, corporate law, I.R.S. forms; and, working without a lawyer and entirely by mail, managed to create our nonprofit corporation and get it recognized on the local, state, and federal levels. Of course, it may have been easier to incorporate in Vermont than in some other states. Vermont in the 1960s had incredibly simple bureaucratic procedures; the state government up in Montpelier was used to dealing with farmers all over the state who couldn't appear in person or afford lawyers or accountants. The hundred acres and houses I bought for $25,000 are now paid off and the property has increased in value many times over. The Monteverdi Artists can live there forever without mortgage payments or rent, although we were *not* exempted from the local property taxes. Having a nonprofit corporation doesn't prevent you from being able to pay yourself and others for services rendered or grants and honorariums, and of course some of the wealthiest companies in the world are nonprofit ones. But all the money must be spent on religious, charitable, or educational programs, and it's surprising how much business can accommodate itself to those adjectives. We could have organized Montana Books, for example, as a religious or educational arm of a church, and thus avoided paying any taxes on our "gross receipts," but we'd have had a rather thin argument for the government. The farm, on the other hand, actually is an educational force, and actually seeks no profit but just a living and a Life.

Another way in which the farm helped me in those years was in providing me thirteen to fifteen dependents to declare on my I.R.S. return. For four years in a row, the I.R.S. accepted my many dependents — all over twenty-one, all with different last names, all unemployed and living with me in my house. They met the legal definition and created such a negative force in my balance sheets that I never paid any taxes. But in the fourth year, when I filed from Japan in ballpoint pen with many figures crossed out and replaced, the long form together with itemized deductions and thirteen dependents — I was audited.

The audit procedure was elephantine, clumsy, slow, and rather stupid. The I.R.S.'s contention was with the high number of dependents. Their lawyers argued that my friends at the commune were not really dependents but were in effect my "hired hands" working for room and board. They cited a precedent case of a farmer in Montana who had hired a widow and her ten children to work on his farm doing specific chores, in return for room and board only, sent them back to their home in Canada after the harvest, and later tried to claim them as dependents on his tax form. But my case was entirely different. My farm was not a "farm" in a commercial sense — it never sold a single peach or can of maple syrup. It was essentially a "private household located in a rural area," and the garden and animals we kept there were for our own consumption of vegetables, eggs, meat, and milk. The people had no specific chores they were required to do. We all lived there together because we were hippies and idealists, and most of us in fact had no income at all.

I took a very innocent and naïve tack with the I.R.S. If in fact I supported all my friends and regarded them as my brothers and sisters (and still do), why shouldn't I be entitled to deduct them as dependents? I even brought my infant son to the hearing and other court proceedings, and he created a *real* distraction with his mashed bananas and little trucks on the floor. He was in a crawling stage. I could have afforded a babysitter or left him home with his Mom, but at this time in my life I never went anywhere where my kids weren't welcome, and I knew the baby would go a long way toward humanizing the rather dull procedure of the audit. You can't very well be pompous and forbidding when some little kid is smiling at you. The I.R.S. took a lien on our house. The people back in Vermont were harboring a person who was wanted by the F.B.I. in connection with 1960s demonstrations, and so were reluctant to fight a court battle over taxes, which would bring more attention to the farm. (The fugitive was eventually arrested but acquitted in court.)

As our court date drew near, the I.R.S. came up with

a compromise for me: they'd give me *half* the dependents if I'd pay for the other half. "Look, I'll *give* you
Linda J—— if you give *me* Marty L——," the man said,
and I laughed out loud. I hadn't realized that the U.S.
government bargained in actual people. I refused the
compromise, but won the case anyway, out of court or
"on the courthouse steps," as they say, as the I.R.S.
simply capitulated on the issue of the dependents. (I
*was* required to pay some additional self-employment
tax.) My lawyer and I, all geared up for the confronta-
tion, were stunned by our effortless victory. We could
only speculate that the government didn't want to *risk*
our winning in court, because that would have set up a
precedent case like the Montana deal. The principle of
the thing could even be extended to a roommate who'd
been out of work in a given year, and might have
sweeping effects on communes and intentional com-
munities. I didn't enjoy my involvement with the
I.R.S., but it's one of those things you can't ignore if it
happens to you. I hired an accountant the following
year and have never attempted to do my own taxes
again. My accountant is a jolly fellow who handles
many writers and artists and is absolutely not worried
or shocked by my financial ineptitudes or "highly
personal" system of bookkeeping.

And government involvements are not always grim.
In 1975, at the peak of our poverty, the city of Seattle
used C.E.T.A. funds to create fifty-five jobs for artists
and writers, and I became a professional "writer in
residence" at something like $600 a month for six
months. Nothing was expected of me or the other

artists except that we practice our art (described in a prospectus which each applicant submitted), but every two weeks a city bureaucrat met me at the bookstore and I filled in a time sheet indicating how many hours a day I'd spent at the typewriter. It was patiently explained to me that it had to add up to exactly fifty-two hours every two weeks. "Let's see, four hours last Wednesday, that makes twenty-seven, and we'll say five hours on Thursday, that makes thirty-two. . . ." The fifty-five jobs drew over five hundred applications, and in one memorable evening the Seattle Arts Commission held an open meeting at which, it seemed, every starving artist in the city got a chance to plead his or her case. So much pleading, so much talenu — and so little help to spread around. There was a coffee urn with a sign reading "Free if you're unemployed, otherwise 10 cents."

And after six months, the lucky fifty-five *were* unemployed again, as the C.E.T.A. funds expired. I decided to try to get unemployment compensation, as F.I.C.A. deductions *had* been taken out of my earnings for six months, but I was told I didn't qualify because I'd always filed my tax returns as a self-employed person. "Well, I'm a *previously* self-employed writer who was an *employed* writer and is now an *unemployed* writer!" I reasoned. And, miraculously, it worked. I had to file claims in the mail every two weeks while waiting through a long appeals process that ended in a hearing with a judge. I was granted my unemployment benefits until such time as the state employment department could find me *another* job as a writer, or until other writing revenues eliminated my need. And the other fifty-four artists-in-residence became eligible as well.

But I *did* notice during this year or so when I was on the government's teat that I wasn't inspired to write much. It wasn't necessary to hustle that magazine piece when at least a minimal income would come in from the endless coffers of Uncle Sam. I've noticed that people on welfare often suffer a kind of loss of self-esteem based on their belief that they can't support themselves, but I'm not advocating the elimination of welfare. Some people need it. Coming off the government subsidy, I tried teaching for a while but wasn't good at it. A raspy-voiced woman called me at six every morning to say, "Can you take Language Arts at such-and-such Junior High?" When I arrived in my classroom, it was as often as not with no idea of what the kids were supposed to be studying. "Hey, Mr. Magoo!" they'd shout. "You smoke hash, man?" My job was to keep them quiet, essentially, and the best way I found to do it was to read them wicked little stories from Spencer Holst's book *The Language of Cats.* "Once upon a time a millionaire playboy burned his face off in an automobile accident. . . ." Total silence. But the principals of the schools objected to Spencer's book, the work was exhausting, and the morning finally came that I told the raspy-voiced lady I *couldn't* take Language Arts anymore. My wife gave astrological readings for occasional clients who came to our home, and a bunch of us created an adult-education course called the Business of Literature (Lit Biz 101), in which we purported to teach others all about writing, bookselling, publishing, et cetera: trades at which we barely made a living ourselves.

I decided to run for governor of Washington State, mostly as a gesture to give myself media space in which to contest the views of our current governor, Dixy Lee Ray . . . "Madame Nuke." Dixy was, of course, the former chairperson of the Atomic Energy Commission under Nixon, and she loves nuclear power plants, nuclear-powered submarines and missiles, and tries her best to bring them to Washington State while people like me try our best to get in her way. It's a noble calling, this politics, only because I know I'm not going to win any election. If elected, I'd turn Washington state wheatfields over to marijuana production and abolish taxes completely. And I have a certain constituency, especially in Seattle, for these views.

Now I campaign for governor all over the country. If Dixy got the job by virtue of the fame she acquired in D.C., I figure it can't hurt my cause to stump in San Francisco, Boston, or New York. In fact, my campaign manager, who's a retired but lifetime Olympia, Washington, state politician, advises me that I should stay out of the state as much as possible. It all started when I was voting in Seattle one day and suddenly realized that your name could be Howdy Doody but you'd eventually get elected to something if you tried hard enough and ran for the office year after year — that's called "name familiarity." From there it was one easy step to thinking that if I ran for governor every term I might get elected by the turn of the new century, the year 2,000, when I'll be about fifty. It didn't seem so far away.

I got on a train out of Seattle one summery day and rode down through Oregon on the platform between the cars, with my head sticking out the window and the wind blowing my hair around. I strolled into the club car and drank three Bloody Marys while talking to an old lady from Phoenix who was with her eight-year-old grandson. The kid had been abandoned on the grandma's doorstep by his mother, and lived with her in Arizona and on trains up and down the coast. A salesman slapped my back and told me all about the dental supplies industry. It made me remember my long three years of weekly appointments at the University of Washington's dental school clinic. San Francisco passed in a dream, Oakland really on the Amtrak route, and even Los Angeles seemed palmtreed, calm, sublime. I switched to the east-bound line and rode the rails out through Arizona and New Mexico. The rainy Northwest had transformed by then into parched, yellow desert — cactus — endless sky. Got off at a small town near Santa Fe and fell into the hospitality of a small band of believers called the Christ Brotherhood, though they denied being Christians and were not affiliated with any church. They operated a free hostel which was open to absolutely anybody and everybody, with beds, linens, and meals. No services. "What a life." What a country, I thought, what a spirit still alive in people! In this country, bad as the economic picture gets, you can still live for free! And we're still the richest people on earth.

In all of my ups and downs in business I was searching for prosperity. I mean real prosperity, which I associate with solid emotional security combined with interesting or inspiring work. The question is not how we spend our money but how we spend our time. All of my mad scramblings for a living were consciously designed to leave me most of my time to write, or enjoy the kids, or travel around in my beat-up VW camper. To make watercolor pictures. To make love. All that I, or most of us, want money for is to buy "free time." Free time is very expensive; it means buying food, shelter, and all kinds of sundries necessary for our comforts while we pursue our craft or art. "Twenty years of schooling, and they put you on the day shift." Your purse determines where you can go, but your time is your life itself.

I still had a long way to go toward that cosmic profit which would earn me dividends every day and put the sunshine in my heart. I took every opportunity to look around me at other people in other places and their businesses, their way of dealing with the problem we've all got of hunger and fear. We fear elimination, extinction — we think we have to fight to survive. You know you're grown up when you start budgeting your time.

# 2
# *Knowledge Is Power*

*". . . the only people for me are the mad ones, the ones who are mad to live, mad to talk, mad to be saved, desirous of everything at the same time, the ones who never yawn or say a commonplace thing, but burn, burn, burn like fabulous yellow roman candles exploding like spiders across the stars and in the middle you see the blue centerlight pop and everybody goes 'Awww!'"*

—Jack Kerouac

I first heard of the Gondt Brothers Cannery in Salmon Bay, California, from a friend in Seattle who went down there on weekends to earn extra money — or, when times were hard, to earn all the money she was likely to get for a week. There was this rusty old cannery, I was told, where everybody working was stoned and nobody paid any taxes and you ate cracked crab on ice and worked 'til the cold got into your feet and your back ached, and got stoned some more to forget it. The cannery operated on the basis of calling in a list of part-time workers when the fish came in and Jim or Phil Gondt had scored a new contract. It wasn't reliable work, and when it did come in, it might be a rush job that required your standing on an assembly line for twelve hours with breaks for joints, beer, and coffee. But the pay was always good, starting at $5 an hour, and the Gondts were famous for treating their employees as family. The cannery crowd was a stoned family business.

When the fish arrived the word spread through the Northwest grapevine of friends and more than once Judy Gondt, one of the wives, called in helpers on no notice of any kind. On one of those occasions I went down to the cannery myself to meet the Gondts and check out their remarkable operation.* It was the beginning of some warm friendships that have sustained me since. I had known rock groups, radical newspapers, and even advertising agencies that operated in a chaotic, stoned fashion, but the idea of a fish cannery fueled by grass and cocaine, moving from empty warehouse to empty warehouse, pulsating with rock music and living outside the law was inconceivable. Almost. But what I found in Salmon Bay was even more admirable than I had dared hope.

People were generally glad to get the calls for workers. Paying work was scarce in Washington state and people went off to California like migrant laborers to accumulate some money and bring it home. But most of the Gondt Brothers' labor force was white, young, and had at least some college. They were the disaffected youths of headlines ten years past. Now they're going back to law school or medical school or opening businesses. Anyway, although there was no glamour to standing on the line tinning crab or salmon, there was also no indignity to it and they were

---

*The names of these people, their business, and their town have been changed to protect them. But they are real people of course, and probably not unique in their *modus operandi*.

certain at least to get high. Because a typical day at the Gondt Brothers began with a group powwow smoking the best dope available, and the entire working day (or night) was interrupted by short breaks for the purpose of getting loaded. On special days, when Santa came the night before, a tiny bit of cocaine might appear, or a lump of Afghani hashish, or some other exotic substance. Beer was always available and free. "If you gotta can fish all day," Jim Gondt said through a two-day-growth beard, "you might as well be somewhere else in your head."

The brothers inherited their father's lifelong interest in fish; the old man had been a fish broker and merchant all of his life. But they acquired the cannery — or created it — in 1971, by which time Jim and Phil Gondt were already professional hippies. Phil's wife, Judy, came in as bookkeeper and office manager, and they made a long list in pencil of all of their out-of-work friends. The list is still hanging on the office wall, with many phone numbers crossed out and replaced by new ones. They started on an investment of under $10,000 with a rented warehouse, cold and damp in the winter, and two arthritic machines that Jim picked up cheaply from another operator who went out of business. They had enough money for the down payment on the machinery and simply hoped to God they could attract the contracts necessary to generate the monthly payments.

In 1977 their gross income was around $300,000, and they had about fifty part-time employees. They've been able to borrow close to $100,000 for new and better machinery through relentless assault on a local

banker. Jim tries always to have a toot of coke before
going to the local banker. Then he puts on his suit and
tie, mumbling, "What a pain in the ass!" "But it's
better than the job I had before we started the business," Jim said; "I was a fish broker and shit, I spent
half of my life in Holiday Inns in Spokane and
Minneapolis and every other godawful city, and the
people I worked with were straight as hell and I had to
smoke dope behind their backs and wear tight shoes
and keep a tight asshole and drink a fifth of vodka a
*day*, man. . . ." Jim said he now has no personal bank
account but he did carry around a roll of cash from
which he paid for goods received, groceries, wages,
advances on wages, loans to employees, and gas for his
1956 Cadillac, which is chauffeured by a seventeen
year-old kid, "Lucky," who used his cannery wages to
buy a huge truck and go into the hauling business. He
simply took care of whatever the cannery people
needed: expansive, robust, eternally grinning, he lum-
bered around the place in jeans and checkered shirts,
propped his boots on the desk of the tiny office (which
has a reversible sign reading "Sorry We're OPEN" or
"Yes we're CLOSED"), and spun fantasies of long sea
voyages off this rocky coast.

The business per se, the skidloads of packed cartons
of canned fish, the fast-moving belts on which the cans
roll to the packers, the machines that pack and seal,
are not interesting even to the Gondts; they understand their machinery but they didn't often spend time
discussing it. What they did do brilliantly was to
manage their resources for the benefit of all the
cannery people by using the rules and procedures of

formal society for their own outlaw purposes. Every cent that came in was spent in such a way that there was no great profit to report to the I.R.S. every April, though in recent years the Gondts have been audited twice and one court case resolved itself with the government and the Gondts splitting the difference between the sum of money each claimed was owed. Phil Gondt called these "unpleasant brushes," and it was clear that he, rather than his brother Jim, did all the worrying about it for the entire family. Phil was the "serious" brother, slim, large-eyed, actually contemplative rather than sober. Jim was nicknamed "the Godfather," and his style was to plunge into debt, make sweeping deals, laugh at the law. But even their occasional involvements with the law hadn't prevented the brothers from expanding beyond the greatest hopes they had for the business at the outset.

Many of the people who worked at the cannery also received some form of public assistance, unemployment compensation, or food stamps. Since their work was, until very recently, sporadic and unpredictable, they couldn't afford to give up their continuing subsidies from the United States. They were paid at the cannery either in cash, which is recorded as wages to "casual labor," or sometimes under a pseudonym, which itself may have a Social Security number. "Hell, you don't need any I.D. at all to get a Social Security number," Jim laughed from across the room, where he was changing the phonograph record. Rock music permeated the cannery at all times. No "person," no legal entity, at Gondt Brothers officially earned enough money to require reporting it on his or her own tax returns. When creditors came to the cannery looking for a specific employee who listed Gondt Brothers as employers and owed money, Jim and Phil simply claimed that the unfortunate debtor was last seen heading up to Alaska in hopes of finding a job on the pipeline. It always worked. I once saw Jim deny any knowledge of the whereabouts of an employee who was standing at his right elbow stacking cans in boxes. "You can always tell a collection agent," Jim said; "they haven't gotten smart enough to come around here in rags."

For the benefit of the straight collection agent or banker, the Gondts turn into reputable business people who appear scornful of their labor force: "Well, you know these people, they come and go." Actually, the workers are their friends, and they, like the Gondts themselves, want to stay alive while retaining maximum freedom. For purposes of a credit reference or recommendation for another job, Jim Gondt made his employee seem a model worker, of course. Life in the cannery was still gritty, still a matter of scamming ways to take advantage of resources so as to work as little as possible. This hedonist philosophy was shared by all, and with great whoops of joyous approval when good times rolled by. And the workers do come and go — that's probably the greatest advantage of the job to most of them. The work is tedious despite good company and anybody who can find an easier way to survive, or who's saved up enough money to hit the road for a while, will do it, and possibly reappear at the cannery six months or a year later with stories of Central America or Morocco.

No successful business is static; it grows and changes like a person, or it dies somewhere in the soul. The Gondts' canning operation grew and grew, and its growth brought with it some new and thornier obstacles to be overcome. They were pressured by the Teamsters to unionize their labor force, but with all the profits of the operation already going into the salaries of the work force, Jim felt the notorious corruption of the Teamsters could only hurt the family sensibilities of the cannery. The employees were unanimously against being unionized; it would cost them dues and most of them don't plan to stay on the job anyway. Wages have gone up consistently as the plant moved to larger quarters, more contracts came in, and the work became more steady. The Gondts were already paying better than any other cannery in the area, and paying in such a way that the employees paid minimal or no taxes and Social Security.

The issue of the union was a delicate one, however. Most of the people at Gondt Brothers philosophically approve of labor unions and the right to strike; without them, of course, the working person might not be much better off than he or she was thirty years ago. But for a beneficent employer and an irregular work force such as existed at the cannery, the union itself looked like almost as much hassle as the government. Unionized workers could not have disguised their income from the F.I.C.A. and withholding taxes; dues would have cut into their paychecks even further; and they'd have ended up gaining the right to arbitrate and strike but losing both the income and the warm, informal association between employer and employee for which the Gondts were justly famous.

As for those occasional brushes, I didn't actually look into the cannery's books (although Jim, characteristically, opened them for me on his desk, saying "Look at our books! You won't believe this!"), but it's clear that the Gondts survived by measures of deceit, good luck, chicanery, and sheer gall—those elements plus the fact that we in the United States are blessed with a bureaucracy that doesn't know what it's doing most of the time. An out-front outlaw shop like Gondt Brothers could not exist in a country like Japan, for example, where the government is efficient and the national sense of honor makes most people scrupulously honest, or India, where it's so corrupt that multiple bribes would be necessary. But the business seemed still small enough to be of no serious consequence to the feds and the Teamsters, and their best efforts to make the Gondts straighten up and fly right were resisted with complete success. The more the cannery grew, however, the greater challenges it had to joust. It's still growing, and every year now it has to adjust its increased volume to an increasingly conservative approach to the outside society.

The cannery grew so fast because it started out so poor and so hungry for work that it was able to service its accounts with lightning speed; gradually, the fish brokers came to know that Gondt Brothers would get the job done faster, if not necessarily better, than its competitors, and at perhaps a slightly better price. This speed in turn was directly related to the instant availability of the work force/family. A Gondt Brothers' clambake or fish-fry party, of which there are several each year, is like a family reunion of as many as two hundred people wildly reveling in fish, good dope, strong drink, and sympathetic company. It's a novelist's Northwoods dream. One time Jim even packed up the machines and a crew of thirty people in huge trucks and drove the whole operation down to Santa Cruz just to service a customer with an urgent need. The guy had tons of shrimp on his hands and no way to get it packaged. Jim charged him three times the normal rate for the special service and put up the crew in motel rooms for the duration of the job — about a week. The guy down in Santa Cruz paid gladly, but objected to the lifestyle of the cannery workers so violently that he wasn't heard from again.

The cannery never operated on any of the new "collective" or "cooperative" bases which other small businesses of a countercultural bent have adopted. We'll visit them a bit later on. From a political point of view, Gondt Brothers was nothing more or less than old-fashioned industry and capitalism operating with the added factor of a kind, even paternal, management. But the sense of real family was warmer, more pleasant, more genuine at the cannery than at any of the cooperatives I visited in my wanderings. For me, Jim Gondt was the heart of the matter — the entrepreneurial daring and genius. It was impossible to imagine the cannery without him, or to miss the point that most of its bold excesses came from his authority and direction.

And, of course, the unimaginable finally happened.

In 1978, the cannery's problems with legal work, debt, taxes, and so forth had grown with the business itself and Phil, the more conservative brother, had felt in the aftermath of the birth of his first child an intense need for the security that would come of going straight, essentially. The work load had grown to the point where the employees were all working full-time and the work was reliable. Under these new circumstances, it grew more and more difficult to avoid the hassles of withholding taxes, Social Security, and the union. It also grew more difficult to avoid attracting attention. Phil found himself living in fear that the I.R.S. would audit the books again; he needed, certainly understandably, the security of knowing that the books would be well kept (no checks for dope!), the taxes paid, the food on the table, and the business firm and unshakable.

Jim Gondt and his brother parted ways — not bitterly or with any legal ramifications, but certainly with some emotional strain. Gondt Brothers had been, after all, the life that they had made for themselves, their family business, their ship of hope. Jim moved his large and outgoing presence to a two-room office in an old hotel down on the waterfront in San Francisco, where he operated a new fish brokerage of his own, called Pacific Star Fish Company. All the old gang came around and things were just as before — Jim with his roll of bills and pouch of magic reefer to blow your head off your shoulders; Jim bailing out some friend busted by the cops for cocaine, agreeing to hire the kid and straighten him out; Jim with a new mustache, a little more paunch, and a pocket watch. The new Fish

Company's just as crazy as the cannery was in every sense, but smaller and quieter. It's an office rather than a huge warehouse, and its only machinery is the telephone. Jim goes down to the docks to bargain with the fishermen. He meets marijuana cargoes up from South America; he's a familiar and friendly figure in waterfront saloons and other places where fishermen gather. "I should never have a business partner, not even my own brother," he says; "I just want to have a goddamn good time and nobody else is going to stand for it."

Meanwhile, up the coast at the cannery, the rock music is still shaking the walls of the new building the cannery has bought. Everything is as before, but the employees work full-time and pay taxes and the whole operation is aboveboard and legal with the exception of the drugs on the premises. Phil and Judy are carrying on the business in the manner that was necessary if it was to survive. Jim has, in effect, started all over and his Fish Company is still small enough to escape detection by the restricting authorities; but Phil is left with the cannery in its eighth year, solvent, business-like, reasonably pleasant but not crazy, not chaotic, not inspired.

I guess a lot of people know the roads between Seattle and California, and all the crazy people in between. The West Coast is certainly growing still, people coming from everywhere else in the nation to take part in the great pageantry of the decline of the West. We'll get to Boston and Maine and New York and all those places in the middle. I'm an East Coast kid myself, and take the grandchildren to visit the folks in Massachusetts every two years or so, but I've been a decade gone in the West and I don't know as I can ever make that winter again. As I'd been living so long in Seattle, the natural place for me to begin my journey into America and my search for Cosmic Profit was down in California, the most populated state of the Union and home of all the freaks who couldn't adjust to life elsewhere. As it was natural for Jim Gondt to move down to San Francisco from Salmon Bay, it was natural for me to head south.

There are actually at least two major roads from Seattle to California, of course — the one that goes along the coast, takes forever, and involves you with many strange characters, and the one that goes inland (Interstate 5), which is fast freeway with identical restaurants and gas stations and very little scenery except for green highway signs telling you how many miles to San Francisco. Most people, including me, take the fast road and forego the endless possibilities — commercial, spiritual, and sexual — along the coast. I've long since passed the age of hitchhiking and taking my chances. Nowadays, I don't go out on the road at all without a car of my own or some plane, train, or boat passage. I hate the idea of landing anywhere without enough resources to take me at least long enough to find a friend, or some work, or some other sustenance.

The approach to San Francisco by road from the north is just as dreamy and sensational as ever, however unbearable San Francisco has become in the last decade. You pass through the wonderland of Marin

County, home of hot tubs and cynical mentalities, and cross over the Golden Gate Bridge wondering over the tossed waves, the impossibly blue water, the incredibly red sky. It's time to find friends and get high and enjoy the boundless fruits of the land which San Francisco, in its occasional generosity to newcomers and pilgrims, is wont to dispense. It's poison to stay in town too long. But a wonderful place to visit, and you can always go out to Candlestick Park with a blanket and experience baseball the way it's supposed to be played, in the sunshine and hopelessly, as the Giants take on the rest of the National League; or go to Oakland and watch the A's flounder about in the American League, stripped of their Reggie Jacksons and Vida Blues by the mad negotiations of owner Charlie Finley, whose Cosmic Profit I'd really love to probe; or go to the opera, the cinema, the ballet, the nude beach, or the Private Party, which is eternally ongoing in this city of the setting sun.

If California's a bit nutty, it's also the birthplace of many new ideas and experiments. It's still easier, somehow, to get across a far-out notion in the Golden State than in most other places. California is currently exporting hot tubs and Jerry Brown to the world. And her "domestic" consumption of every material thing is awesome, particularly in L.A. It's still a kind of Disneyland of wacky sights and sounds for people who come from more sober places.

I pulled off the highway at San Rafael, just north of San Francisco, expressly to meet the lady who had saved my feet. My feet were saved by something called the Birkenstock sandal, which is a distant third in competition with Earth Shoes and Root Shoes in the marketplace of "natural" or New Age footwear. The New Age is for the most part a commercial conspiracy by now, but the Birkenstock company in Germany is actually two hundred years old and still run by the family. It's amazing, then, that the sandals were not available in the United States until 1967, and that in 1977 only 100,000 pairs were sold in this country — giving Birkenstock a gross around $2 million spread over 300 retail outlets. Its headquarters in San Rafael includes 2,500 square feet of modern warehouse space and a small, brightly sunlit office with four desks. The lady I mentioned is Margot Fraser, who started the business in gratitude for the sandals, which eased her foot problems.

But to backtrack just for a moment, for some reason feet jumped into the natural arena a few years back and made millionaires of a few people with new ideas. The most noticeable success was Earth Shoe, which employs a recessed or "negative" heel concept. The Earth Shoe brochures explain that the designer, Anna Kelso, who is an elderly Danish yoga student, had the inspiration for the shoe during yoga exercises in Santos, Brazil, in 1957. Walking on the beach near the yoga monastery, she dug her heels into the sand and achieved a "standing yoga position" which she claimed aided breathing and posture. She became convinced that nature intended us to walk that way — uphill, so to speak. Earth Shoes were introduced in Denmark in 1960 and launched in the United States on Earth Day in New York City in 1970. They've been a hit ever since, although some people can't wear them because they put stress on the Achilles tendon, which in turn can cause leg, neck, and back pains. A clinical study, aided by a grant from Earth Shoes, conducted by the California Podiatric Medical Center in San Francisco in 1976, estimated that 30 percent of the people in this country can't wear Earth Shoes because they have very flat feet or Achilles tendon problems. Millions of people do wear and praise them, and Earth Shoe had 200 United States outlets selling its products exclusively by the end of 1976.

Roots were designed by Don Greene and Michael Budman, who founded the Don Michael Company in 1973 and had sales of $10 million by 1975. They were in their mid-twenties at the time, and designed the shoe with the help of a Polish family of shoemakers in Toronto. Roots also employs a negative heel, but with a more moderate angle than that of Earth Shoe, and they also feature a sole that is 65 percent rubber and 35 percent synthetic. Earth Shoes' soles are only 10 percent rubber, and Roots believers say their shoe is more natural and offers more "give," more of a cushion to the foot.

The most *natural* shoe, apparently, is the Space Shoe, which is custom-designed to fit your own particular feet. Robin Zehring described the process of getting fitted for Space Shoes in *California Living Magazine* as "exciting, sensual, and a lot more fun than having a dentist fit you for false teeth." You sit in a "throne" chair while plaster molds harden around your feet for almost an hour, then wait two months for the Space Shoe factory in Bridgeport, Connecticut, to produce your personal shoes, which conform to every curve in your instep and are said to be of heavenly comfort and incredible durability. The price two years ago was up to $125 a pair. Space Shoe is "far and away the best that the most money can buy," according to Zehring.

Most of us can't afford Space Shoes, and barefoot is the only really "natural" way to go. The next-best thing to barefoot, for me, proved to be Birkenstock sandals, which run from $8.95 to about $35. The "footprint sandal" has a cork innersole, soft and malleable, which adjusts gradually to the exact shape of your own feet. Each pair of Birkenstocks eventually acquires the shape of your footprint — not a recessed heel, but the natural bends which posture presses on the soft earth. You can't, in other words, wear somebody else's pair of Birkenstocks, and your own pair slowly becomes as comfortable, nearly, as going barefoot.

But Birkenstock sandals look funny, and that definitely keeps some people away from them. I've heard them described as "like a pair of big, floppy snowshoes." They're loose and oversized and they *do* flop around, because they give you the most possible space for your feet. Any kind of shoewear is going to restrict your feet somewhat, but with Birkenstocks the general idea seems to be that loose is good. You can't wear them to the opera or any formal occasion unless you just don't give a damn what anybody else thinks. But they're so comfortable that once you start wearing them, it's pain and trouble to wear anything else.

Birkenstocks seem particularly attractive to people

with chronic foot problems, which I had until I found them. I stumbled into them because a young New Yorker named Melanie Kornfeld brought them to Seattle in the form of a tiny Birkenstock nook located in the back of the Growing Family health-food store at Green Lake. The Growing Family was one of those communal health-food stores which was so loath to make a profit that it went out of business after seven years because "nobody was into it anymore." You had to weigh your own produce and tea and herbs, and slice your own cheese, and order your raw milk a week early. They were always "out" of a lot of things, and when you finally assembled your food order at the cash register, you had to hunt up somebody who would ring it up. It was a great place to shop, though, if you had small children (which I usually did), because they could play on the warm rug in the kiddies' corner with all the offspring of the other shoppers and with various toys. And you had to have all the time in the world to meander, chat, meet your neighbors, and so forth. The Growing Family was more of a social club and well-spring for exotic religious ideals than a grocery store. The Family has occupied a couple of big ramshackle houses in the Wallingford district for years, and finally, of course, organized their nonprofit foundation and acquired a ranch in the mountains.

Anyway, Melanie's little Birkenstock nook was a "business" in name only for the first couple of years, because she sold fewer than one pair a day on the average. Melanie originally came to Washington state to go to college at Bellingham, and ended up doing her schoolwork all day long at the Growing Family, waiting for her one or, on great days, two customers. The absolute profitlessness of the business didn't faze her ardent belief in the sandals. Melanie even sold people sandals on a pay-later, return-guarantee basis. She'd offer to take the sandals back after a month if the customer wasn't completely addicted to them, and of course no sandals ever came back. She patiently proselytized. And, to make a long story short, Melanie's Birkenstock store is today located in one of those jazzy new "malls" on Seattle's highly commercial University Way and she's finally selling Birkenstocks in real volume. She even opened a branch store up in Bellingham.

Margot Fraser supplied Melanie Kornfeld with Birkenstocks. She started importing them from Bad Honnef on the Rhine in '67 on the smallest of scales, beginning with one retail outlet — the San Rafael health-food store owned by Howard and June Embury, who eventually became her partners in the distributorship. Like Melanie, Margot started with a $25-a-month rented nook in the health-food store, but the demand for Birkenstocks was small and she had to return to her career as a fashion designer. For a period of eighteen months in the late sixties the business went adrift and no Birkenstocks were imported to the United States. Today she works out of the new Jacoby Street warehouse and manages a small staff of people who, like herself, "had personal problems with our feet." She is soft-spoken, almost academic in her approach. On the day I met her she was wearing conservative but brightly colored clothes, loose sandals, of course, and a pair of funny socks which enclosed her toes, separately, in multicolored sheaths. Margot Fraser could pass for an Opera Matron. She promotes the sandals in small, personal ways — such as fuzzy reprints of her article, "The Crimes We Commit Against Our Feet," from *Let's Live* magazine — and advertises them only in special publications devoted to health. She reminded me of Gen MacManiman in her almost-maternal concern for my feet.

"Leonardo da Vinci called the foot the greatest engineering device in the world, and he picked the word *engineering* rightly," Mrs. Fraser said. "*Just think* of the resilience and tensility of the foot — its capacity to support an enormous amount of pressure per square inch. Think of a ballet dancer's ability to focus her whole weight on the muscles of one toe!" Our feet are "the hardest working part of the body," she said, but most people are somewhat ashamed of them, and keep them covered in symmetrical shoes which don't match the foot's natural shape. "If we want the naked foot to be beautiful, we'll have to forget the notion that the dressed foot should look *small*."

The footprint sandal allows the foot to resume its natural shape, with a straight line on the inside which permits the big toe to align naturally with the heel. "You could straighten your feet with exercises instead," Margot Fraser offered; "but if you do five minutes of exercises a day, already you're a hero, right?"

Carl Birkenstock, the current president of the company, is in his forties and gets most of the credit for the footprint sandal, which the family introduced in

Europe twenty years ago. His father and grandfather made arch supports. He knows Margot Fraser, of course, because she goes to Bad Honnef at least once a year on buying trips, but Birkenstock himself has also visited the United States and met some of his small-time dealers. Of the 300 outlets in this country, only 25 stores are exclusively Birkenstock-stocked; 165 are health-food stores, 120 general shoe stores, 75 boutiques. The average shoe store starts with an inventory of $30,000, the average Birkenstock outlet with under $10,000 total investment — and not all of it in inventory. "We chose to stay with small specialty or gift shops, rather than the large department stores," said Margot's partner, June Embury; "because we seemed to do better in the little stores where the people would wear the sandals and become personally enthusiastic about them."

"Our success depends on the product, but also on the people who sell it," Margot added. "We are *all* fanatics."

The business has doubled in size every year since 1971, when it grossed only $35,000. One senses in Margot Fraser's calm and intelligent approach a simultaneous absence of any greed, hard sell, or grand expectations, *and* a kind of quiet confidence and faith in her ultimate success. "We are tiny compared to Earth and Roots," she said softly, "but we think we're the comer because the shoe really holds up to its promise. People who can't wear a negative heel can wear Birkenstocks, and keep coming back for more."

While bombing around New York City subways, I noticed that *Time* magazine was promoting Earth

Shoes in poster ads which announced that the shoe "fits" in its pages. Birkenstocks, at least to date, have "fitted" into the pages of the most esoteric publications for health nuts. "Our success has come entirely from word of mouth testimonials." One gets the feeling that if Birkenstocks suddenly hit it big and the business became intense, competitive, and anxiety-ridden, as almost all big businesses are, a person like Margot Fraser would retire from the scene. Everything about her is relaxed and easygoing, and such people don't end up at the top of corporate hierarchies, at least not usually. She could pass into a position like chairperson of the board, an honored post as founder and inspiration, but she'd have to leave the selling, advertising, marketing, and shipping to more aggressive types. (This is not to deny the commercial value of sincerity and honesty, but we live in cynical times and I am quite sure that Margot Fraser could not be as pleasant and easygoing as she is if the moderate success of her venture got out of hand.)

She also feels good because her feet feel good. If your feet hurt, as we all know, nothing seems right. "One of the first men in modern history to recognize the bad effects shoes have on health was Father Kneipp of Germany," she said. "He had his patients take off their shoes and walk barefoot in the soft grass, still wet with the morning dew. They came from far and wide to get relief for their fatigue, general debility, and nervous exhaustion. He merely removed the causes of their trouble, and nature, always tending towards perfection, did the work of restoration.

"A hundred years later," she continued, "this is still

the best advice one can give for foot health: walk barefoot as much as you can. But be sure it's on natural surfaces which cushion the foot."

I walked out on air, but only to be accosted and brought down by a woman in the parking lot who was selling pyramids. I obviously liked Margot Fraser and her shoes and I value Birkenstocks more than I do pyramids. California's crazy; you can sell anything. People will always be searching for the perfect shoe, Margot had said, because "you can replace your shoes but not your feet." Her business is grounded in quality and durability. The pyramid industry, by comparison, exists on a popular intellectual notion which could pass out of fashion. We're all fanatics, all fans, all faith. Pyramid freaks publically claim that the mere presence of a scale-model pyramid, usually made from "pre-energized aluminum tubes," in your house or office will make you feel, think, and sleep better. They are said to make plants grow taller and more healthy, to facilitate deep meditation, to create "greater life-energy fields," faster hair growth, relief from pain, and accelerated healing. Whew. A company called Nick Edwards Environmental Systems, Inc., in San Francisco, has a brochure on Pyramid Energy which sums up the case:

> Just as a lens collects and concentrates light, or a television antenna captures the T.V. program you wish to watch, the pyramid shape collects and focuses the gravitational/magnetic field that swirls over the entire Earth. We call this force Pyramid Energy. This energy has a beneficial effect on all

living things and a preservative effect on non-living matter. Scale model replicas of the Great Pyramid of Egypt, when aligned to Magnetic North, trap, focus and resonate Pyramid Energy. This energy is collected by the pyramid shape and discharged from the top (apex).

I met this guy at a kind of New Age environmental fair (spelled "faire" of course) who walked around with a pyramid on his head. He uttered soft-spoken truisms and homilies. Pyramid Energy. The Great Pyramid itself covers 13 acres and rises to the height of a 40-story building. People who have been inside it report that their minds achieved new heights of meditative bliss or that it was dark and cold or that their guide overcharged them. Ten miles away, in Cairo, some of the worst urban decay and human suffering in the world goes on . . . and on. Paul Horn, the jazz flautist who'd become famous when he issued a record of music performed inside the Taj Mahal in India, took his flute and machinery into the Great Pyramid and made a sequel there. I interviewed Horn for a magazine story at his hand-built oceanfront home outside Victoria, British Columbia. We looked at color slides of the Pyramids and drank vodka and listened to the haunting music.

Scale-model pyramids start at about $5 for a six-inch base and climb up into the hundreds of dollars for elaborate "Dream Machine" matrixes, huge mobiles, "sleep systems," meditation models. Naturally you get more pyramid energy the greater your pyramid *is*. Which means the original one in Egypt generates worldwide. And it is tempting but difficult to believe in pyramid energy, if only as an alternative to nuclear power.

San Rafael, Sausalito, Mill Valley, Berkeley, Oakland. Even the names of the places called up memories of endless excesses in my past. But this late-seventies life is nothing like the past. Even the madness of California is businesslike. I picked up friends as I went along — writers, photographers, mystics, and saints. Berkeley is professionally stoned, which doesn't prevent it from being expensive; the cradle of the Free Speech Movement in 1963, it once housed its population in doorways, on the street, in funky backyard cottages which could be rented for $50 or $100, in forever-parked VW vans with madras-cloth curtains and psychedelic graffiti all over the side. Today, the typical Berkeley backyard cottage is worth $75,000 and rents for $550 — first, last, dep., no kids, pets. Home burglaries are so common that formerly liberated types have to get into all kinds of security precautions. Even Patty Hearst wasn't safe. The place now has a dangerous edge; it's more the city and less the sleepy, sunny outlying town it once was. But it's still probably the most progressive and tolerant city in the country, a goldmine of unusual business and certainly, I hoped, a place where some people must have found real happiness and satisfaction, real profit, in their work. A sea of artisans, craftspersons, dealers in metaphysical notions, artists, writers, derelicts, professors, inventors, delinquents, and degenerates. I was glad to find my old friend Berkeley still grinding away.

Having loaned out the car, I found myself climbing into the shabbiest taxicab in the world on Telegraph Avenue. This trashed old Pontiac with dents and green paint splotches probably dated from the era of the Free Speech Movement itself. The driver, Marty Kaminsky, turned out to be an old comrade from some movement demonstration in Boston. As we careened through the streets of the capital of the revolution, like Hanoi in its new commerciality, Marty invited me to a meeting of his company's drivers and I learned about Taxi Unlimited. It's an "anarchist collective." In fact, when anarchists can form a collective, what do words *mean?* It has about 20 part-time drivers, but only four cabs, four permits, and *three* insurance policies. The company doesn't check the meter; "we all just trust each other." When passengers are "cool," a fair price can be negotiated and the meter not used at all. Your Taxi Unlimited driver is a friendly freak who's even more open to outrageous arrangements than ordinary cabbies would be; he or she will take you anywhere, make a good deal on the price, and maybe even take you with the cab to places you didn't realize you wanted to visit. Take a T.U. and you're going on a trip.

All the cars are blown-out reconstructed junkers, like the Rent-a-Wreck cars in L.A., which movie stars and all kinds of people rent (very cheaply) to be inconspicuous! T.U. is an exercise in negative chic, an organization which seems to keep running despite the universal distaste of all its members for organization itself. T.U. gets hassled by the authorities. And we go up and down Telegraph like czars of the New Age economic trust. Transmissions grind and scrape, tires blow, and you never know what's going to happen next. The nipple lady passed us, dressed like a huge nipple and selling plastic stick-on nipples in all sizes. Bands of chanting Hare Krishna heads rounded the corner at Durant. All the specialty stores selling rare and pornographic comic books, hashish smoking and cocaine cooking supplies, popular music records and instruments, vegetarian and purist foods, posters and books. Every major intersection had palm readers, Tarotists, and astrologers offering on-the-spot analyses. I ducked into the cool recesses of Shambhala Booksellers. It took over the Christian Science Reading Room's location on Telegraph in 1968, and in case you haven't noticed, the Christian Scientists always get good spots.

Shambhala, like the Christian Scientists, is a spiritual organization, and all the books in its store are more or less esoteric adventures in zen, Buddhism, astrology, Sufism, Arica, est, Rolfing, Tibet, etc., etc. The *air* in that place was pregnant with some Kabalistic awareness. It was quiet, cool, and dark after the turbid scenes on the street. Too quiet, in fact — I was sure that I remembered it as once being busy and caught up in the rapture of new discoveries. The bookshop offered lectures and programs, of course, then branched into Shambhala Publishers, which was so hugely successful that its entire catalogue of titles is now distributed by Random House. But — something was different by 1977, something missing. And *someone:* Sam Bercholz, for years the most public genius and general director of Shambhala, and now spending his time in Colorado and Europe and where-all on the heels of his master, Tibetan lama Chogyam Trungpa.

I spoke with the store's manager but didn't stay too long, as he seemed busy. As I suspected, he confirmed that business in the store had gone down since reaching its peak in the early seventies and he cited "an overall decline of interest in metaphysical books." "Many of these books are now turning up in general bookstores with occult or metaphysical sections," he said, but "the real depth of the market is in specialty stores like ours — we attract people who really want to get into it."

I wasn't that serious myself, so I slipped out and over to Shattuck Avenue to check up on KPFA, the West Coast's first public radio station — listener-sponsored and far left of center — and my old friend Larry Bensky, who was then KPFA's program director. The door was locked and operated on a buzzer/intercom system, just like New York City. But once I got inside the studio, it was clear that KPFA hadn't changed. Bensky was sitting under a mural of muscled colored peoples rising up against their oppressors, talking into two phones at once. He was wearing his knit blue cap with pompom over the bald spot on his head, and his hair came out at all angles down to his shoulders. Somebody was ranting about Rhodesia over the air, and promising an upcoming program of Balinese music, and a gay men's show called "Fruitpunch." The station's been operating continuously since 1949 and still has to cajole and plead with its listeners for their subscription funds. "C'mon, we're sure you're out there, and if you subscribe now you can get a free year's subscription to *Struggle* magazine."

I feel more comfortable with the politicos than with the metaphysicals, while carefully declining to join either in their groups and movements. I sat in Bensky's incredibly cluttered office while people came in and out whom I'd met in Washington, D.C., New York, or Boston. Ah! I made a tape of myself reading from one of my books for later broadcast. KPFA was the flagship station of the Pacifica network, mostly FM noncommercial stations in the larger cities. It operates on a measly $500,000 a year, Bensky complained, but has a large staff and a good range — 59,000 watts. Nobody who works there is paid as well as his or her skills could command from a richer station, but there is still a great measure of idealism at KPFA and people like Bensky still work there, despite chaotic and stressful lives, because they believe in the place. Nothing could be finer than to be in California and listening to KPFA. Unlike most media, it makes no pretense of "objectivity" in its news or features. It's an outfront would-be revolutionary station which really feels its debt to the community. If it's sometimes annoying to hear people yammering away about the "Third World Gay Caucus Convention," it's more than compensated by the exotic music and news which more closely matches my points of view than CBS or NBC ever will. KPFA makes sure you know about what the oil companies are trying to foist off on us next, how badly the prisoners are treated in the jails, how unfair the society is toward minorities and women, and how to watch out for paraquat in your dope. It can be depressing, but not any more so than ordinary news.

From there, I tore over to the El Drisco Hotel in San Francisco for a wild dinner scene and party, which ended with a retired CBS record executive, who had turned into a wandering minstrel complete with accompanist and costumes, hugging the waiters and leading us all in a dance up the street. His name was David Kapralik when he was producing records by Bob Dylan and Sly and the Family Stone, but now he calls himself Ilili. He operated his joy missions out of an elegant home in Hollywood Hills and took his show to orphans and retirement homes. Obviously, Ilili was losing money in this kind of show business, but Ilili was clearly having a hell of a good time at it. "I put away my peanuts," he sang, "and I re-tired, got new tires, and now I'm rolling again!" Ilili was white-bearded, festooned with jewelry, covered from head to foot with medieval dress. His laughter filled the Vagabondo Restaurant. He invited me down to his house, which was neighbor to Doris Day's and the late Freddie Prinze's, and I later took him up on it, staying in a velvet guest suite and being woken up every morning at noon by a manservant named Saint George with black coffee and croissants on a tray. I sang him my version of Rodgers and Hart's song "Moon of My Delight," and he urged me to cut a disc. But I drank too many Black Russians and forgot to do it.

I staggered forward into San Francisco society. I

discovered the Years Ahead Custom Hair Design studio in S.F. and its sole proprietor, E. Graham Baker, a thirty-year-old entrepreneur who came into the business with a considerable family inheritance behind him. Years Ahead conducts a "search for the perfect haircut" while operating on the basis that each of its hairdressers "owns" his own chair in the shop: that is, each pays the company for the privilege of working out of its stylish facility in the city, in the heart of the Polk Street hurdygurdy which has absolutely succeeded New York's Bleecker Street as the nation's gayest neighborhood. Each carries on a kind of personal trade within the framework of the organization. But the company is owned by E. Graham Baker himself, who does not cut hair.

He lives in a palatial Pacific Heights mansion near the stately El Drisco Hotel (a story in itself with littleoldlady tenants and wicker furniture and breakfast at which individual slices of bacon and toast are sold, and the hotel stationery proclaims that "Never has a life been lost with such protection!"). He has callers and he makes deals. I happened to visit a few days before Christmas, and found him dwarfed in his enormous armchair by the biggest home Christmas tree I've ever seen. And I *believe* in Chrsitmas. Where I come from, you buy the tree from the local Boy Scout troop at a vacant lot near the supermarket for $20 down to $2 on Christmas Eve. The early afternoon light hurt E. Graham Baker's eyes; he was just out of bed and looking as hungover as a millionaire playboy should. He barked orders at the servant — answer the door, answer the phone, for Christ's sake — while describing Years Ahead's "spiritual work in the area of healing."

Hairdressers "take karma out of their clients and take it into their own matrix, where they are unable to transfer it through the pool of consciousness," Baker said. This accounts for what he describes as their typical neuroses. He started Years Ahead as a gift to his partner, Marty Allen, who "got himself murdered in October, 1974," when he attempted to resist a couple of Latino teenagers who were holding him up on the street at 3:30 A.M. In its first year, under Allen's direction, the salon was chaotic; it had "problems of how to operate without a lot of agreement in the world." Today, it is "cleaned up, quiet and making money, but I'm not going to get rich at it!"

The purpose of Years Ahead "is to serve people by designing their hair so that it serves their purpose in life . . . so it's appropriate to who one is. Get your hair out of the way and let yourself come through. San Francisco itself is about 'being yourself.' " The business "reaches out to everybody" but "of course it's easiest to get the gay trade." A short visit to the salon itself made everything even more clear. It is dazzlingly beautiful, coldly chic. "The gay trade" in San Francisco is both well-heeled and socially first rate. What it does not have is any sense of family warmth; it would be closer to the truth to say that each of the hairdressers is in competition with the others, and all of them are in debt to E. Graham Baker. Who, back home, is planning to expand the business into national marketing of a natural shampoo he's invented "from the basic chemistry of the body."

I left Years Ahead, taking with me only a Christmas card with a poem in it, written by Baker and distributed "to all my personal friends everywhere." The poem was about light and giving and sharing, and concluded with—a copyright line. God forbid any "personal friends" should reproduce it without written permission.

I woke up the next day in Sam Matthews's Victorian parlor in Stinson Beach. *Two* rather imposing grand pianos. Stinson Beach is a resort town only 20 miles north of San Francisco, but approachable only via a tortuous, twisting road that winds through Muir Beach and Mill Valley and other paradisial Marin County scenes, and Sam Matthews is a young book entrepreneur who is in no way rich enough to own the house or the pianos, but who is charming enough to be the Bay Area's leading house-sitter. House-sitting is an art and profession which demands a whole book of its own. Ever since I first met Sam, in 1971 when he was touring the East with Alicia Bay Laurel, whose book *Living on the Earth* Sam had published under the imprint of Bookworks and later sold to Random House, he has always lived in other peoples' homes with consummate grace and style.

Anyway, Sam and I got pretty loaded that morning, and he started telling me stories of his early days at Bookpeople, the now-famous Berkeley book distributors, who are a kind of clearinghouse for small-press publishers and kinky new notions. At the beginning, Bookpeople was a scratch operation open to crazies, but the spectacular sales of such California-based small-press originals as *The Whole Earth Catalogue* helped it to climb to its present volume of $4 million annually and a staff of 35 to 40 full-time people. Despite its nouveau corporate-collective structure, which effectively prevents anyone from making a personal profit, ego-based power struggles within the organization shaped its current hierarchy, Sam said. Bookpeople's glossy catalogues sell some 600 small presses to the bookstores, and many of them owe their entire distribution and very existence to it. People have said that you can't really launch a small-press book anymore without the help of Bookpeople.

That's an exaggeration but Bookpeople is certainly one of the most successful of the "collective" or group-benefit companies, and was worth a visit — even though I had personally experienced a little war with Bookpeople over Huxley's *Art of Seeing* and found myself just one of many small publishers who have beefs about the distributorship. Rumors fly, and I'd heard literally hundreds of arguments for and against Bookpeople, and took all of those mixed feelings with me in my first visit to its warehouse. I picked up a writer friend, Paul Williams, somewhere north of the city, and together we invaded the huge warehouse in the dusty back streets of Berkeley. Fortunately we found that, once we were inside, the good feelings and attitudes of the people overrode our reservations and, in my case, the bitter memory of the squabbling over the Huxley contract, and we felt very much at home in short order.

Terry Nemeth met us at the door and escorted us around the place, and I finally got acquainted with a face to match a voice I'd heard on the telephone many times. Actually, Terry's voice was different because he was suffering from flu, but he was bravely supervising the empire with Kleenex box in hand. I toured up and down endless aisles containing all the books of Brother William, Black Sparrow, Dustbooks, Capra, Cloudburst, Blue Wind, Whirlwind, Garden Way, Kinkos Graphics, Linga Sharira Incense Co., Oyster, and Over the Rainbow presses. Bookpeople now accepts only one out of every 25 small-press titles submitted for distribution, Nemeth said, which means that its staggering inventory is only a tiny fraction of all the cheaply published stuff floating around out there. You could say that publishing one's own book has become a major hobby, or pastime, in America, even though very few of these efforts reach a comprehensive readership. It takes major funding to make a movie, but anybody can turn out a "book" of some kind for a few thousand dollars and hope that a major publisher will pick up on the rights.

Bookpeople "buys" the books from their publishers or creators at a discount of about 60 percent off the list price. But their standard arrangement is a consignment deal, by which the books remain the property of the publishers while they sit on Bookpeople's shelves, and are considered "sold" only when they leave the warehouse. Three months *after* their sale, Bookpeople pays for them, but it demands payment from the booksellers within one month. It definitely makes exceptions to these arrangements for the major publishers, some of whose books Bookpeople also carry, and this favoritism toward the more creditworthy big publishers, while reasonable and businesslike, still angers some of the small presses who feel toward Bookpeople that it's not just another distributor but something of their own, something of a family of progressive people which exists *mainly* to boost the circulation of small efforts. What happens to the small press is that it ships its books to Bookpeople in January, the books don't start going out until March or April, and small checks start coming in in July, August, or September — by which time their dollar value has been seriously eroded by inflation.

But Bookpeople itself, like all book distributors, is waiting for its payments and operating on a profit margin of only a few percentage points. Most of its employees own at least some shares in the company, but the shares must be sold back to Bookpeople at the same price at which they were bought when the employee leaves the job. In other words, there's no way for one's investment to grow, and, in fact, it depreciates because the dollar does. It was hard for me to understand why people would buy stock that is guaranteed to go down in value, but the only answer is that they obviously enjoy working for Bookpeople. The scene there was lively. The place buzzes with new ideas and social trends, and the company uses the increased business to improve its job benefits, which already include free lunch, medical and dental insurance, and an icebox always full of cold beer to be consumed on the job. The shareholders have democratic meetings, so every one of them feels some voice in the direction the company is taking. More business means better wages and working conditions, but the whole system depends on a great deal of trust and honesty on the part of the people who work there. Every one of them has to take a proprietary attitude toward the stock to protect it from "shrinkage." As with Taxi Unlimited, nobody at Bookpeople seems to think it's a problem. And one real advantage of its kind of ownership, which leaves no person with the odious responsibilities of being the "owner," is that nobody has to be tormented by carrying the weight on his or her own shoulders. Most of the original Book-people people, like Sam Matthews in his mansion, have left the company for other horizons. The institution marches on with a changing cast of characters, and I had to give it credit. I don't think there's another distributorship which operates on quite such a level. Bookpeople's major competition, RPM Distributors in Maryland, was organized on an almost identical basis but went out of business in 1977. Bookpeople now offers the best hope for a small press or self-published book to reach a wide bookstore audience.

South of San Francisco, in Millbrae, I found another publisher more or less comparable to Bookpeople in size, but owned by a more conventional corporation, headed by Hal and Ruth Kramer. The Kramers call their press Celestial Arts, but started twelve years ago as the Orbit Printing Company; as of 1977, Celestial Arts was producing forty original new titles a year, which made it "the only legitimate trade publisher on the West Coast," by Hal Kramer's claim. Hal and Ruth are middle-aged, middle-class people with a deep interest in publishing and making money at their business, and their clean, quiet, spacious plant was nothing like Bookpeople's long-hair paradise. The Kramers have hired some of their top editors directly out of New York firms, and so built a reputation for Celestial Arts as a kind of West Coast East Coast publisher.

"Trade" publishers publish books in cloth and high-quality large-size paperback bindings, intended for sale in general book and other stores; the adjective "trade" distinguishes them from mass-market and textbook publishers, whose books are sold in supermarkets and college stores and other places outside the "trade." Celestial Arts' titles have focused around the "human potential movement," new health practices, meditation, spiritual teachings. It's done very well with the sincere poetry of Walter Rinder, whose sentiments appeal to millions of readers. "We've *got* to do the far-out thing every time because nobody else in New York is going to do it," according to Celestial's editor, George Young, who came to California from a huge mass-market firm. I checked my notes twice to see if he really said "nobody else in New York," one of those telling slips we all make — as if Millbrae, in its sunshine, was really a neighborhood of Manhattan, an extension of Madison Avenue.

Hal and Ruth were worried about the future for the kind of hip publishing they're into. As printers, they had begun with psychedelic and antiwar posters, which sold so well in the sixties that they turned available capital over to books by Alan Watts, Laura Huxley, and others from the mainstream of "new thought" in this nation. But you really can't see the

Kramers sitting zazen in some temple or eating organic muffins as hard as hand grenades, and they don't pretend to lead the lifestyles toward which their books are definitely aimed. "It's worrisome that we *don't* know," Hal said, "just what new ideas people are going to adopt. Our choices are always based on intuition alone. In the case of an Alan Watts or Walter Rinder, say, we succeed, but other books don't do nearly as well." George added that "the future is kind of muddy right now. The best people in publishing are walking around with question marks on their faces."

It's true. Crazy stuff that would seem to have a very limited audience can take root and sweep the country, while other books never find their fans. . . . I am speaking specifically of ideas in the psychological or religious realms. Every year seems to bring new self-help methods which purport to help you clear your guilty conscience, make more or better love, raise your children wisely, or simply achieve enlightenment and bliss. Millions of people go in for the new trip, the new diet or mantra, authors and gurus get rich, and then, usually, the fad passes. Trying to pin down some permanently valuable ideas or really substantial writing talent is such a subjective thing that a publisher is always taking a risk. "We are living up to our image at this point," Hal said, "which is one of trying to be responsive to what people want to read." Celestial Arts feels, even in its relative security, like it is experimenting, taking a chance, working with untried design and production ideas and unproven human-potential ideology. I couldn't help hoping that it thrives.

Of course media people, whether in books, movies, magazines or newspapers, *live* on new ideas. The pressure to find them which the Kramers felt is multiplied many times over in the offices of slick monthly magazines, whose editors are, or can be, embroiled in a frantic search for the latest word. But I got a little tired of words and booktalk and decided to go out and meet some people who work with their hands. California, as everywhere in America, is jammed with craftspersons selling their wares — potters, painters, jewelers, sculptors, leatherworkers, knitters, bookbinders, makers of sterling-silver cocaine spoons, etc., have turned up on streetcorners and in public markets and flea markets, and you can only assume that some of them are making a living from their homework. Work of an exceptional quality turns up alongside the most miserable amateurish efforts. The street people I chatted with pretty much gave the impression that there is only the scarcest living to be made in crafts; but once the artist is established, he or she can work on consignment for individual clients, get off the street, and possibly do much better. I'm sure no accurate statistics are available, but who knows how much business there is in this country in cocaine spoons? (Or for that matter in dopes themselves? I haven't addressed the issue of marijuana dealers here, because marijuana stories are already very common, but this group may be the largest self-employed bloc of all. The San Francisco *Examiner* in 1978 concluded that marijuana is the third largest business in the nation! Literally billions of dollars are going around in cash in that trade, and since they're not bank-accountable or taxable, the United States Treasury is reportedly experiencing massive discrepancies in its accountings of where the money goes.)

Jaime Tapley was known as Lazarus Quan for most of the years since he left his Florida home at sixteen, a precocious and clear-eyed runaway, and arrived in Washington, D.C., for the 1968 Poor Peoples' Campaign. He was your smartass kid of that era, too bright to stay in school, articulate and at ease in any social situation. We let him move into our house, from which we also published a daily nuisance called Liberation News Service. (It was a nuisance to *us*, not to our subscribers.) Lazarus was good on the press, on the collating machines, the addressograph; he seemed to have a gift for making things work. He figured to compensate for his lack of a high-school or college diploma by learning a craft, "a trade." To suit Lazarus, who demanded that life be gracious and elegant, even beautiful, it had to be a little-practiced, ancient but honorable art. He settled on hand bookbinding, and learned it from elderly masters in Vermont, eventually establishing his own workshop in Montague, Mass. In 1971 he brought the rig out West and today he lives in a San Francisco apartment crammed with heavy book-presses, long tables, reams of Japanese marbled papers, binding tools, and binds precious books for affluent clients and whole press runs for publishers. His work is good and his services in demand; people like to rebind their family Bibles and old books, and some people collect fine bindings for investment purposes. Jaime had part of a leg amputated in 1974, so the health of his home industry makes his life easier. He has to get around the city only for social purposes, and can work and make a living without leaving home.

But Jaime Tapley is not Lazarus Quan, sixteen and free to roam; he's twenty-six and tied down by tons of equipment. When he moves, it takes trucks. When he talks about the success of his trade, it's with a trace of regret. He can't get away for the weekend because he's working on a big job from the Boston Public Library. He stares into San Francisco Bay from his parlor window, and he seems to have Morocco, Greece, and Sicily on his mind.

Down the coast in Carmel I met Ephraim Doner, a well-known artist whose engraved tiles are now so famous that he's made them for the homes of such celebrities as Linus Pauling and Joan Baez. I ended up helping him one day as we moved the heavy boxes of tiles from the workshop, where they'd been fired and cast and painted, to the billiard table outside his pleasantly wooded home on the way to Big Sur. The ocean danced in our eyes. "It's not only the ocean, man, it's our future!" Doner enthused. "We'll stay around here and haunt it after we're dead!" Doner is in his seventies, a short, rotund, white-bearded Russian Jew who speaks in six or seven languages, can and does converse about art, music, the great books, and he dances, spins like a whirling dervish, embraces everybody he meets, and generally pours incredible energy into the world.

I asked him about the tiles. "Ah yes, the tiles! I do think they get better every year. Actually, I'm a genius!" The tiles are highly prized, close to indescribable: figures with outstretched arms to the moon, fishes, fawns, gnomes, Hebrew lettering spelling out "If not now, when?" He works on them every day, bound in a grey potter's apron from North Carolina, and breaks open a special bottle of wine to celebrate every night. And dinner with Don, as he's called, and Rosa Doner, his wife, is always an unforgettable occasion. Their kitchen and fireplace are lined with the exquisite tiles; oil paintings of their parents; a large canvas of Don's exploding with light; for a full portrait of the scene, see Henry Miller's book *My Bike and Other Friends*, which has a chapter devoted to Doner. I surely loved the man.

Down in Hollywood, with Laura Huxley in her home on Mulholland Highway, we were drinking champagne while massaging our feet on rubber pads with upright bristles that tickle your soles and reputedly encourage good posture and circulation. They felt good, certainly, though I could have ascribed my general euphoria to the charming company and bubbling brew. We visited Laura's sprout-tray farm and dined on little green shoots, then were served a tray of vegetarian bacon strips called Stripple — crisp snack treats which tasted astonishingly like bacon and are made of God knows what. Something supposedly better for you than pork. What will they think of next? I'd spent the day tracking down Famous Amos, the tall black genius who'd created Famous Amos chocolate chip cookies, at $3 a pound the best c.c. cookie in the world, and trying to make sense of the transfer of the

L.A. *Free Press* from its original owners to Larry Flynt, publisher of *Hustler*, who then named Paul Krassner, the notorious, as his editor before being shot in the South. Krassner appeared at a party being given for a book publication, said, "What are *you* doing here?" with a great grin, and I replied, "Haven't got the faintest idea." And realized it was time to leave California.

California is a giant plum for the picking. As of late 1978, she had record low unemployment and record numbers of people, and they're still coming. The business pace is careening straight ahead. The dollar goes down in Europe and everybody panics because the stock market follows suit, but when the dollar goes *up* abroad, it forces a recession at home. Inflation is the number one concern, and real estate values even in earthquake-doomed areas are astronomical. Jerry Brown surveys the wacky scene and calmly announces, "All part of the mosaic."

# 3
# Misery
# Loves
# Company

*"Business is divine activity."*
— *Ralph W. Emerson*

The city of Boulder is located in north central Colorado approximately twenty-seven miles from Denver and forty miles from Rocky Mountain National Park. I loved it as a young man. It was high, cool, a haven, a safe place. Ten years ago, when I first visited Boulder, the "Summer of Love" was underway and the town was, or seemed, full of sunshine, hope, and love. It was a college town with something more, some magical quality of bringing spiritual belief into play as a function of ordinary life. Exuberant mystics, hippies disconnected from all responsibility and employment, runaways from middle-class homes, bemused academics, self-proclaimed revolutionaries, dope dealers, writers, artists, musicians: these were the street people of Boulder. We believed we'd found a place without industry, a kind of free territory (like Berkeley, Ann Arbor, Austin, Cambridge) for the freaked-out multitudes. We believed in "free" in those days, it was our most common and beautiful word, everything had to be free, but most of all life itself had to be free. We lived on love and acid. But, for most of us, anyway, the ideology soured as we grew older and learned that *nothing* is free, we can't even lead our own lives unless we can find the money to support it. You're free only if you're willing to live without personal possessions, without a house of your own or a car or anything but clothing and a few personal effects; with that kind of light load, I find, people can still exist on the margins of middle-class society without being unhealthy or undernourished. For most of us, though, a stable home is the least of our needs, we're tired at the end of the day, and we'd die without the comfort of a private space, a home.

The street soothsayers of 1967 predicted that a great flood would engulf the United States in 1968, and that Boulder, a mile high, would be one of the few places to be spared total devastation. Of course they were wrong. But if we understand the "flood" as a mental or spiritual danger rather than a literal, physical one, there may be something to it. Boulder is not inexpensive anymore — it's commercial as hell — but the spiritualists are thicker than ever. It's a religious town; everybody believes like crazy in something or somebody, and even the business sense of the town is saturated with philosophical posturing.

I blew into town on a cold spring wind. It was already warm and pleasant in Seattle and California, and I came to Colorado in my Birkenstock sandals without socks, which footwear had to serve me as it snowed twelve inches and the streets and sidewalks were covered with solid ice, later with freezing mush and rivers of melting snow. I'd left my winter coat behind, and had only a small wool jacket. And I didn't feel I knew anybody in town *well* enough to ask to borrow boots or a coat, whereas a decade earlier I would have petitioned a complete stranger. The "free" people are gone, of course, and the housing squeeze is on, and I wasn't carrying money enough to outfit myself with new apparel.

But it wasn't long before I ran into the same Christ Brotherhood organization that operates the free hostel in Santa Fe; they'd arrived in Boulder with plans to recreate their New Mexican operation in this, the capital of New Age finance and spiritual business, and I met them on the steps of the post office. They offered to put me up at their house in the hills outside town and I knew I could prolong my stay in Boulder if I didn't have to pay for a motel room, so in the next minute I was in the back seat of a really failing Toyota or Datsun — the thing was barely running — with a couple of long-bearded guys, a woman in nineteenth-century dress, a few babies, a dog, some groceries, spare parts, paperback books, and we were winding out of Boulder headed toward the mountains. The house was at the end of a long, perilous road, and was a very clean, warm, comfortable and glowing scene of domestic tranquility. Pictures of Jesus, candlelight, sacred music. The women cooked, cleaned and took care of the babies — not to the exclusion of the men, who were also tender toward the children, but it was clear in some mysterious way that the old-fashioned division of labor on sexist lines was still alive in these dedicated people, was not offensive to them. The men chopped the wood, brought home the bacon, led the sacred readings at the dinner table. It was an intentional community, I've known hundreds of them in my life but not in recent years — I'd gone the way of the nuclear family, living with just my wife and my own children in our own house in Seattle, living the life that I once scorned as the plague of the bourgeoisie and the source of the loneliness and confusion in modern life.

It started to snow — hard. It was the first week of April, 1977. I had at least a warm place to sleep and nourishing vegetarian food, but I knew it was a long way back to Boulder in that broken-down car, and that the snow on the road could make the trip impossible in a matter of hours. The Christ Brotherhood wanted me to stay, permanently if I would, their chief asset in business was people, not money, and when they found someone with energy they went after that person as a businessman goes after a contract. Their business was to give away material things to the poor, to anyone who asked, all they wanted to do was open free hostels all over the world, and although they never begged it was clear that their financial support came from the occasional wealthy believers who'd donate to the cause. They had faith that they would receive exactly what they needed, and so lived without security in a teeming, wondering mass and charged blindly forward into the cold world.

Jesus Christ was their banker and you can't help liking Jesus Christ, but He makes me nervous. You don't have to look very far to find people murdering each other in His name. So-called Christians build deadly nuclear weapons, and apparently being a Christian in this country doesn't prevent you from doing much at all.

The people of Christ Brotherhood would undoubtedly agree. They were wary of other Christians, organized ones, I mean, and they believed that their own organization was distinct and different from the others. They did have piety, though, and piety always makes me want a brandy. I slept the night in an impeccable shrinelike room and found the next morning a lot of snow on the ground and no particular eagerness in the group for a trip to town. The idea of staying another day without strong drink, without at least the *possibility* of sex, and without furthering my pursuit of Cosmic Profit made me crazy. I resolved to walk the twenty miles into Boulder on my Birkenstock sandals, and when my friends saw that I was serious, they relented and we drove into town, skidding and sliding down serpentine mountain roads, and I went off to study businesses after arranging to meet them at a given time and place, knowing full well that I would give them the slip. I thought I had to do it that way since my rational arguments fell on deaf ears, when I'd say that I had to live in town to do my work they'd cheerfully promise to drive me back and forth daily, and that was that. I felt imprisoned by the Lord. Now I was walking through the snow in the sandals *and* skulking around corners in fear of meeting up with the fervent Christians again; but Boulder is a small town and of course I did meet them again, and found them *forgiving* of me. As we forgive those who trespass against us.

I decided to try out the Green Mountain Grainery

health-food store first, remembering that as a friendly community-gathering place of years past, and found it was still a haven of a sort. Within a few minutes, I'd talked myself into the manager's office and was relaxing on the couch making phone calls and eating honey ice cream and drinking organic root beer. The Grainery has long had that "loose" feeling; people who popped in and out of the office didn't seem surprised to find me there and we exchanged small talk. One of the store's directors was living in the offices with his two-year-old son while searching vainly for an apartment in Boulder, so there were diapers and toys everywhere and a general feeling of home in a business context.

Ten years ago, when the Grainery opened on Arapahoe Street, the customers and staff were sunny, tenderly young people who struck out for a healthier diet in the spirit of revolutionaries. The store was small but had a sophisticated selection of natural foods, a superb tea collection, and "natural" Nat Sherman's cigarettes from New York City. By 1977 it had vastly expanded and was doing about $2,000 a day in business, had replaced the simple cash registers with computerized models, and exists as part of the Green Mountain Grainery, Inc., a corporation which distributed and manufactured cookies, trail mix, and other health foods and grossed about $1.5 million. None of that had apparently changed the basically sleepy, friendly feeling the place has. It's a place to post notices on the bulletin board and meet friends, etc. I knew I could work out of the Green Mountain office and that somebody there would help me find a new place to live, even though I had no formal connection to the company and when I arrived didn't know anybody who now works for it. In the store's back delivery-parking lot I got into a conversation with a guy which nearly landed me a decrepit Datsun for $200; fortunately, I had enough cowardice in me to dread the vision of the thing breaking down partway to Seattle, and I didn't have the $200. One of the clerks in the store introduced me to a smiling macrobiotic couple whose home up the street was eternally open to wanderers, and I moved into their living room to sleep on a mat on the floor. It wasn't as comfortable as the Christ Brotherhood house, but at least it was in the heart of town, free, and the macrobiotics never tried to convert or proselytize me. They weren't even home most of the time, and they didn't lock their doors. They didn't smoke dope or drink, and of course they didn't eat anything except brown rice and vegetables, so I carried on all my habits outside and retreated to their house for peaceful sleep at night. It was a step off the street when I most needed it.

The big idea in Boulder is to go talk to Mo Siegel at Celestial Seasonings, because of all the hip businesses this company is perhaps the best-known and most widely admired. It's also fabulously successful. With $9 million in sales and about 200 employees by 1978, it has an energy to grow that is continually *burning*. Most of that comes from Mo Siegel. "Siegel," wrote Jesse Kornbluth in *New Times*, "has visions of Iced Red Zinger (Celestial Seasonings' most popular tea) displacing Coca-Cola in the hearts and minds of America's young." There's no reason to think that

Celestial Seasonings will ever stop growing, if Siegel has his way. But Mo is also, in the best tradition of Boulder life today, a religious leader, a man who talks God all day long, who puts his aggressive corporate development in terms of serving God and the people, who holds a "prayer and share" session in his office with his employees, who denies that making money is important to him, who claims that he hires people he is in spiritual communion with. His particular scripture is something called the *Urantia Book*. He signs his letters with blessings and continually invokes the almighty as he charges into whirlwind expansion, schemes constantly to outdo his competitors, fights off unions and employee complaints and writes the company's high-toned soft-sell advertisements. There are about a million Mo Siegel stories, and dozens of magazines and newspapers have covered Celestial Seasonings' meteoric rise.

Celestial teas come in bright, psychedelic boxes, and until 1977 the teabags were attached by a thin plastic strip to a tag with a wise or humorous saying: "Avoid middlemen, deal directly with God," for example. The tags were eliminated following a huge flack from workers and customers about their nonecological plastic strip, but Mo certainly also realized it was cheaper to produce the tea without them. Some customers complained, and I can remember people buying up the remaining cartons of Red Zinger or Pelican Punch with the tags. Now the cartons offer short philosophical/spiritual essays on the side, and the familiar Celestial Seasonings invitation for customers to write in their concerns and ideas. Siegel offered me $50 for every such piece of "universal truth" he could use on a tea box, and he gleefully answers spiritual and personal questions addressed to him through the mail.

Siegel is now twenty-nine years old and started the company when he was twenty-one, with Wyck Hay, his co-president. At first it was a homespun enterprise which gathered herbs in the hills outside Boulder and packaged them in hundred-pound burlap sacks for bulk sale. The company didn't make money but gave Mo and his friends an outlet for their passionate interest in herbs. In fact, Mo and his wife, Peggy, had cooled on the business, he said, when they traveled to Ecuador in 1970 to find a guru named Dr. Love-Wisdom, who turned out to be a mad hermit whose "spiritual community" was a fiction. They returned to Boulder and threw themselves into work, as many people do when they return from fruitless pilgrimages. I spent a year and a half in Asia myself before returning to the United States to get married and start a business. Nobody in India had the degree of cynicism about business which exists in this country, and the idea of making money was no longer taboo in the face of starvation.

I'd read somewhere that Mo rides his bike to work (it was in *People* magazine) and on bad weather days has been known to hitchhike, often being picked up by one of his own employees. I had no such luck, and as the Boulder bus system wouldn't take me to Celestial Seasonings' warehouse, I had to walk it through the slush. But Jeannie Turner, Mo's secretary, gave me a warm welcome and saw me outfitted with hot Mellow

Mint tea (not just mint, but alfalfa, licorice and other treats in a pleasing blend) and a tremendous mountain of printed literature about the company to occupy my time while we both *hoped* Siegel would reappear. He steams in and out of the office without warning, like a firestorm, and there was no predicting when, if ever, he'd return. He spends a lot of time in Third World countries gathering herbs and spices and arranging exports, and he refuses to make appointments in advance. (I'd tried that from my phone in Seattle for months.) "Oh, God, I'm afraid you've missed him," Jeannie said with real disappointment for me in her voice. I wasn't worried because it was warm in there, smelled like mint and chamomile and sage, and I had all day. When a few minutes later Mo appeared at the door grinning under his mustache, in blue jeans and checkered shirt, and spoke about ten words before racing off again, Jeannie brightened. "Mo's back," she said.

Mo's qualities of spiritual leadership don't leave him invulnerable to attack. The workers call him "Schmo," and at the All-Company Meetings some of them invariably arise to attack. In 1977, the big flack was over the Iced Red Zinger, which required nonnatural ingredients to achieve its fruity flavor, and the purists held out for organic beverages while Mo dreamed of taking on Kool-Aid and Coke. Everything's relative in business as in life, and Celestial Seasonings has to be seen as small compared to General Foods. Mo isn't shy about saying that he wants to take on the giants, either; he's hired the Colorado brokerage firm of Boettcher and Company to help find new investment capital for massive expansion. Mo got his Iced Red Zinger through in a modified — still not 100 percent natural — form, but he appears to be losing the 1978 issue of South African rooibos, which he wanted to blend into a new tea called Emperor's Choice. An anti–South African uprising in the ranks put the rooibos aside, at least for now. The worker poll went two to one against it. But Mo was later quoted in the San Francisco Bay *Guardian* saying, "Maybe when the heat is off this South African thing, I'll just use it anyway." The tea-baggers once shut down their shift to petition management about the irritating effects of tea dust in their eyes and lungs. Mo introduced new technology to solve the problem. In fact, something's always new at Celestial Seasonings and the place seems in a constant turmoil.

Jeannie and I toured four buildings in all; it was, or seemed to me, a conventional plant full of assembly-line production in all departments and mammoth storage facilities for teas and herbs from all over the world. Celestial has had to deal with increasingly intense surveillance by the Food and Drug Administration, which has more than once held up or condemned tons of tea on the grounds of "filthy" or "unsanitary" things in the ingredients — including bird and other unidentified excreta, beetles, aphid legs — all to a degree that was unacceptable to the feds. Celestial Seasonings counters that the alien-substance percentage was a tiny fraction of 1 percent, and at that natural "alien substances," which may occur in shipments of chamomile, are preferable to the chemicals which are legally contained in ordinary teas. Actually, the FDA has no established standards for herbs like chamomile but its inspectors have a broad authority to hold up or condemn shipments if they find them unsanitary. There are periodic attempts to unionize the work force, but Mo pointed out that he admires I.B.M.'s corporate management, in which hundreds of thousands of employees are not unionized, and he vows to defeat the unions by providing more and better benefits for his workers than any union could demand. These benefits, or "perks," include a free communal lunch, bicycle races, Celestial logoed T-shirts and hats, and the development of an employee shareholding system. But wages at Celestial Seasonings have never been high. A tea-bagger now makes as much as $4.70 an hour or as little as $3.00 an hour, depending on production efficiency. That the employees are not afraid to voice their complaints when they feel like it makes Mo's vision of the company as a cosmic spiritual community all the more progressive. A woman on the bagging line said she wouldn't work in Boulder if she didn't work at Celestial Seasonings. To make it there, you have to work for something more than money, some inner peace which comes from providing the world with its needed natural tea, some spiritual aim. You have to keep your goals and ideals high when you're making three bucks an hour. It helps, I imagine, to believe in Mo Siegel, as he seems to do in himself.

We talked in bubbles of a few minutes at a time as Mo ran around the office. He seemed very concerned with the federal government and its excessive power, but his arguments were not substantially different from those you'd expect to hear from any industrialist. "Big government interferes with business," etc. But he always added that he loves the bureaucrats as his fellow men, that he couldn't assume they were bad in their hearts. "Or in the pay of the big food corporations." While he railed at government, he insisted that he's not worried about it, that everything would work out, yes, just as the Heavenly Father meant it to.

Mo was promoting his bicycle race, the Red Zinger Classic — *Sports Illustrated* had written it up one year with the warning "Red Zinger, sports fans, did not pitch for the Toledo Mud-Hens in 1935" — and the company volleyball games, a new brew, including nonherbal black teas, which contains *more* caffeine than coffee and is called Morning Thunder ("with the power of a thousand charging buffaloes," Siegel wrote), and his new solution to crime in America. It's all based on Love. He handed me a copy of the guiding principles of Celestial Seasonings corporation: it was like being given the Ten Commandments. Number One is "to do the will of our Heavenly Father (more widely known as God)." (Some of the women complain about the Father bit as sexist, but obviously Mo doesn't care if you choose to view your Father as your Mother, it's the same God.) Number Four is "to encourage and uplift family living at home and throughout the world." (Anti-gay?) Number Six is "to be motivated by service rather than profit." And Number Seven is "to develop within the next decade a sales volume of many millions of dollars per year, employing many people and distributing products that will directly aid the health and welfare of the planet."

But, said Mo Siegel, you also have to keep a sense of humor. Oh, yes, and you have to have advertising!

Mo had a Jewish father but was raised in a Catholic boarding school. He lives with his wife and their kids in an ordinary house on an ordinary street in Boulder. His raging ambitions for the company have not affected his personal lifestyle, and he wears a three-piece suit only when going off to talk to "straight" investors. "We're returning the idea of play to work," he said. "What we're really about is the fatherhood of God and the brotherhood and sisterhood of man." Then he blessed me and I blessed him right back.

Crazy town, Boulder. It always makes me feel a bit lightheaded, could be the altitude. But they do mean business. Pearl Street has been restored with a new pedestrian mall and many bars, restaurants, discos, and shops selling the latest conceits for the affluent campus types. They have an Old Chicago restaurant, which is built around a Chicago motif, with 1968 Riot Combination pizza and a Chicago Seven pizza with seven ingredients. For two dollars your waiter or waitress will smash a pie in your or somebody else's face, complete with a bib. The Brillig Works Bookstore, which started as a woodsy, homey bookshop, had prospered and expanded and been sold to the new owners. Eastern religion may be the biggest business in town. Nobody's willing to divulge the extent of the holdings of Tibetan lama Chogyam Trungpa, Rinpoche, but they include the Naropa Institute, whose illustrious faculty draws thousands of students to Boulder for classes in meditation, Buddhist studies, zen, yoga, Tibetan

studies, Freudian psychology, theatre, gestalt, modern
art, flower arrangement, dance, poetics, physics, biolo-
gy, and music. The teachers include Allen Ginsberg,
William S. Burroughs, Gregory Corso, and Ed Sanders,
treats for Beats and would-be Beats, also Gregory
Bateson, Fritjof Capra, John Ashbery, Meredith Monk,
and Jean-Claude Van Itallie. Most of them teach the
occasional seminar. Naropa is organized as a nonprofit
Nalanda Foundation, of which Trungpa is president
and chairman of the board of directors. As the Institute's curriculum and physical facilities have grown,
claiming whole blocks of student housing and classroom buildings, it's not as ridiculous as it sounds to
imagine Naropa Institute one day surpassing the
University of Colorado at Boulder in enrollment
figures. When Trungpa is in town, his many disciples
glow all over the streets. When he's giving a lecture,
excitement is in the air. He is also certainly the
guiding light of Shambhala Publications, which moved
from Berkeley to Boulder to consolidate with him,
according to Sam Bercholz, its founder. Sam now
travels with Trungpa around the world. The one place
they *can't* go is back to Tibet, which Trungpa fled in
1959 with a daring escape from the Chinese. "The
Chinese Communists," as he calls them. Since then,
he's been in the United States generating passionate
disciples and wild tales of high life, sports cars, binges
in the New York City night. He is said to have ordered
Ginsberg to shave his trademark beard, and Ginsberg
complied. I saw him once only, when he came to
Seattle to institute a new center on Vashon Island,
Washington; he answered questions from earnest

students with sharp, sarcastic rejoinders. They apparently enjoyed his divine ridicule, which did have a special sense of humor to it, but I missed the point, I guess. Doesn't matter; to each his own guru. Rennie Davis, who's one of the original Chicago Seven (can you remember all their names?) and was always a sober and serious political theoretician, went crazy for Guru Mahara-Ji, said he'd "walk across the country on my knees to kiss his feet," and had settled in Denver to sell earthworms (Planetary Earthworms) and, later, insurance for the benefit of the guru's Divine Light Mission. It's amusing, though, to check out the reduced-price remainder books in Boulder, which provide an index of fallen saviors, who may have been selling like wildfire the year before. Having gotten only printed matter and evasive answers to my probing for dollar figures at Naropa and Shambhala, I decided to give up on Boulder religion for a few hours and plodded across the U.C. campus to see a movie, *Gone With the Wind,* for a dollar admission. When I emerged many hours later, like Scarlett O'Hara swearing that I'd never be hungry again, it was dark and freezing. I walked back to my mat with my head hangin' down.

I continued to take advantage of the good graces and warm hospitality of the Green Mountain Grainery as a kind of local office in Boulder, and that led, of course, to my looking into the Grainery's own meteoric rise. I was beginning to think, though, that I should be investigating businesses that went under or failed if I wanted to find happy people who'd found Cosmic Profit. The successful businesses all had some degree of stress and aggravation to level on their managers and employees, and people like Mo Siegel, who seemed to thrive on problems and always laughed them off, were rare. I went over to Green Mountain's warehouse to meet Bruce MacDonald, one of the vice-presidents, and found him surveying ten-foot-high totem poles of packed peanut butter ready to be shipped. But it took nearly two hours beyond our appointment time before I could get his undivided attention. I sat in the tiny office, the only warm place in the building, and tried to get my socks and sandals to dry out while plowing through more catalogues and brochures, of which I'd accumulated a small mountain since coming to Boulder.

MacDonald was the nervous, chain-smoker type. In fact, a lot of executives in the natural-foods industry whom I met smoked more cigarettes than I did, and I was at the time consuming a pack a day of Nat Sherman's brown "pure/natural" Cigarettellos. The natural-foods industry is a giant; it is consciously preparing to take on the food establishment of America, to invade the supermarket shelves before the regular corporations can come up with more ersatz natural food like those breakfast cereals with outdoorsy names and logos and a ton of white sugar in 'em. It is in a furious, uncontrollable state of growth, and only those with considerable tolerance for paranoia and competitive idea-making need apply. The biggest problem, MacDonald said, was government intervention, a complaint I had heard so often from hip businessmen that I thought I was in some right-wing party.

I earlier explained everything that I know about government from personal experience. I haven't been exposed to limitless hassling; usually I just stay out of their way and they don't even notice me. But the mention of government started MacDonald on a tirade. "In ten years government will *crush* all small business," he said. "Every area of business is regulated to various degrees already. The telephone is a monopoly controlled by government and no longer based on innovative management . . . in some sense, free enterprise is in better shape in Russia!" And so on. He recommended I read *Atlas Shrugged*, by Ayn Rand. "The U.S. government services you as little as possible, yet they tax you coming and going."

Green Mountain got started in the wholesale food trade with granola, that ubiquitous breakfast crunch which mothers of America are now pressing on their children who'd rather have Apple Jacks, and the company "grew in spite of itself" thereafter. Celestial Seasonings grew *because* of itself, but Green Mountain is a good example of what can happen when you take the plunge. One thing followed another — "everything we did in the early days turned to good — because of the timing." The company set up an Art of Living cooperative, instituted a stock plan for employees so generous that the employees now control the stock. "The reason we're successful is that the whole universe is coming to us," MacDonald enthused. "We maintain a level of integrity with regard to our quality. The business is infallible as long as it's well-managed."

"But," he added, "we have no intention of becoming

one huge concern under one corporate name." It'd be better, he thought, to break the business down into divisions, keep it personal, "small," as invisible as possible to the bureaucrats. Aside from the feds, MacDonald worries all the time about competing natural foods wholesalers: "You wouldn't believe the paranoia level in this business, man," he said; "people steal ideas. I have to be careful of what I say to you. I can't talk about our new products until they're out there." A competitor, whom MacDonald refused to name, actually strongarmed health-food stores into refusing to stock Green Mountain's products even when its prices were lower. He became angry and bitter. He went to bed at night, I thought, worrying about some bastard or other who's trying to horn in on the market.

Which is, in fact, exactly what happened. Expansion caused a philosophical and financial crunch at the Green Mountain Grainery corporation. It has all but gotten out of the wholesale foods business, and has been decentralized to the point of selling the Grainery stores, most often to the people who have been managing them. The company seems to be coming full circle — back to the small, "family-owned" business it once was — but with a twist: the Grainery plans to franchise its name, and the expertise it has acquired in ten years in business, to "families" anywhere who can pay the fee.

Natural foods is still a relatively new field, and is still growing in popularity among the consumers. The situation now is not unlike one in which pioneers and adventurers, having discovered a new territory, begin to carve it up and give it names and save it for their grandchildren. What happens in the next ten years will determine which firms are going to survive in the cutthroat natural marketplace, and which will be absorbed, squeezed out, or crushed by federal harassment. Think of *that* the next time you're munching granola.

Finally it got dark and started snowing again, and MacDonald rushed off in a gleaming Green Mountain van, one of a fleet, while I pondered, and walked the streets some more. Decided to try the bars, pick up gossip, see who was around. The bars of Boulder are full of white kids who've never known hunger or a day's work in their lives and a sprinkling of eccentric characters who have just arrived from Europe or India or down from the hills in jeeps. Some creeps. Many holy or religious personnel, many holistic and natural leaders, all tying one on. All exercising their freedom. Squandering the fruits of someone's labor. I ended up in a roaring saloon talking to John Steinbeck IV, the novelist's son, or more properly yelling at each other over a table littered with pitchers of beer and downed glasses of whiskey. We went off to his house and I gave up my macrobiotic mat for a couch in Steinbeck *fils'* living room; we talked and talked all night.

John had written a book called *In Touch*, about Vietnam, a pretty good book, too, which like most first efforts didn't create any great stir or wind up on the bestseller list. He seemed to think it was a tremendous disadvantage to be the son of a famous writer if one has writing ambitions of one's own. The most touching thing I can remember from those days of excess and final descent into Boulder Decadence was his description of being in an expensive boys' prep school with his brothers and feeling inferior because the other kids were sons of doctors and industrialists, and had more pocket money to spend. "There we were in this fancy school, y'see, because my father believed in *education* but his books weren't making *big* money in those days, you know, and it took everything he had just to pay the tuition, and sometimes he was late on that. All the other kids had cars and clothes and money to spend going out, and we were just *humiliated*, man. We couldn't really fit into that society. It was a drag to be the son of a writer." I swallowed hard. I send my own kids, who are just tiny tikes, to private schools the tuition of which exceeds my house payment; and I'd been late on the tuition payments more often than not. But I told myself, as Steinbeck *père* undoubtedly did, that my kids were getting the best possible educations. (And of course they're too young yet to care much about money.)

Lessons, dancing lessons from God. I left John sitting in bed watching a Perry Mason rerun on afternoon T.V., and slogged my way out of town, to the airport, and away.

It reminded me of the lines from Lord Byron, with a New Age twist: "Let us have wine and women, mirth and laughter, / Sermons and health food the day after."

# 4
# Blood
# Is
# Thicker
# Than
# Water

*"The intellect of man is forced to choose*
*Perfection of the life, or of the work,*
*And if it take the second must refuse*
*A heavenly mansion, raging in the dark.*
*When all that story's finished, what's the news?*
*In luck or out the toil has left its mark:*
*That old perplexity an empty purse,*
*Or the day's vanity, the night's remorse."*
*— W. B. Yeats*

I went back to the West Coast and decided I needed a bodyguard to accompany me on my next trip out; not to actually guard my body, of course, but just to be a friend, somebody to talk to in strange, cold towns at night. The perfect traveling companion was Jim Gondt, the cannery man down in Salmon Bay, and it didn't take me ten minutes to convince him to drop everything, pack up some cocaine, and set out with me for Minneapolis and Saint Paul, the twin cities. It was the summer of seventy-seven, and we figured to hit a number of towns stretching from Minnesota to Maine, poking around businesses and looking for a good time. Jim and I entertained each other with stories and

110

slipped off to the airplane rest room for quick tokes of Colombian weed, drank Bloody Marys, and landed in Minneapolis ready to tear up the streets. Judy Thompson, my partner in Montana Books in Seattle, had moved back to Minneapolis, her home, and met us at the airport in a long dress and sandals like some midwestern farm wife; what a joyful reunion!

Minneapolis is one of those cities that's perfect copy for inflight airlines magazines and travel books. It's been working overtime for years to generate culture and art and sophistication in what is essentially a raw midwestern sprawl, freezing in the winter and broiling in the summer and just a hell of a long way from anywhere else. But it has the marvelous Guthrie Theater complex, which produces about four hundred plays annually, lots of nouveau downtown architecture, restored Nicollet Mall, a superb Children's Theater Company, the first and largest consumers' food cooperative in the country, and thousands of craftspeople, artists, and cottage industries, as well as giant corporations. If you can stand the weather in Minneapolis, it's friendly, open, and receptive. It reminded me of how Seattle had seemed five years earlier, before its secret got out.

Thanks to Jim's connections, we somehow ended up staying in the plain railroad flat of a Minneapolis cocaine *aficionado* and between Jim and this guy there seemed to be always a small mountain of the white powder on the kitchen table, and we all tooted it morning, noon, and night. It might be worth a moment here to marvel at the cocaine business in this country. Nobody knows why, but in the last few years it's gone from a luxury drug, available only rarely and only to the very rich, to something that regularly appears at middle-class parties, on college campuses, in the ghetto, even (the newspapers rumor) on occasion in the White House. Cocaine is no longer endemic to a narrow subculture but is widely used and discussed and yet is still *so* illegal that in most courts a cocaine conviction is a guarantee of Doing Time. In other words, some of the most respectable people are willing to risk a great deal for their felonious delight in the stuff. They're also willing to pay $100 a gram, which can be easily snorted up by two people in one sitting, and to risk being burned by impure stuff that's cut with talcum powder or whatever. But the coke we had in Minneapolis was the purest I've ever experienced and was free — a requirement for me, because I've never paid for coke; it's out of my financial reach — and it seemed never to diminish. We had planned to stay for a few days and ended up spending a week and a half, and every moment of it charged with the inhuman energy and delusions of power and grandeur which truly dynamite coke will bring on.

Some people do fare better with it than others. In my case, coke always has bad aftereffects, physical and psychological pain which can be relieved only by more coke. In other words, I think it's addicting even though this point has been argued back and forth, and it may be *less* addicting to some other people than to me. Anyway, although it gave us a great ride and people in Minneapolis are still talking about those ten days in July when the coke never ran out, it also left me with very dim memories of what actually happened.

I do recall visiting the Minneapolis Peoples Food Coop, which was the first of many food-buying cooperatives in the country and is still one of the busiest and most progressive. If you live in any major city in the United States, you probably have a food coop and know the score. You pay membership dues, which entitle you to a lower price on the groceries and a vote in the store's periodic meetings. You're expected to weigh and bag and even price various items by yourself, and the clerks don't necessarily know the latest prices on everything. Most of the stuff is organic, natural, or produced by small enterprise, and therefore more expensive than its counterparts in an ordinary supermarket, so that even with the membership discount counted in, it's seldom cheaper to shop at the coop, but you can congratulate yourself on eating organic peanut butter or real goat's milk or high-protein bread. At the Minneapolis coop you can also buy nongrocery items, attend seminars and meetings, give away kittens, find an apartment or a job, or fall into some exotic religion. It is all things to all the people: they own it and use it just as it uses them.

And we did drive over to Northfield, Minnesota, to meet a lady named Margaret Bakke and see her company, Banbury Cross, which makes toys out of Marimekko fabric from Finland — in stunningly bright colors and outrageous geometric designs. Maggie's original butterflies, hobby horses, and stuffed animals are sold in fifty-five or sixty retail outlets, just enough to keep her and from one to three other people employed year-round in a gutted old red-brick mill.

Northfield, Minnesota, was lost in a pastoral dream. Most of the college crowd was away on summer vacation, and the dense green foliage left the place in a jungle-like torpor. The air was sweet with the smell of flowers. It was a perfect day to swim in a lake, lie back in a lounge chair, drink beer, eat peanuts, and watch a baseball game on T.V. (The day before, we'd gone out to Bloomington to watch the Twins play the Baltimore Orioles, but one of our party, a carpenter from Colorado who was trying to adjust to life in Minneapolis, went berserk behind the coke and booze and we had to leave in the fourth inning with this screaming maniac in tow.) But fortunately the atmosphere at Banbury Cross's studio was relaxed as the day itself. We found Maggie deep in production for the Christmas season, for which she designs new toys every year. Her clientele is limited to "progressive small toyshops" and her reputation is based on personal references. We found ourselves surrounded by fantastic Marimekko cloth toys by the thousands, an adult Disneyland. We visited the next suite of rooms, which belonged to a talented stained-glass maker named David Kjerland. The old mill would eventually be filled with craftspeople — none of them rich or famous but most making a living and smiling. A bunch of them joined us in a backyard barbecue which turned into another great, roaring party.

Back in the city, I spent some hours talking with Bruce Lansky at Meadowdale Press, which has had three or four titles on the bestseller lists out of a small family-owned center in the suburbs; and met Brian Anderson, editor of the city magazine *Mpls./St. Paul*,

"The Magazine of the Twin Cities," which was involved in a war with a competing mag called *Twin Cities*, the publisher of which had sued to prevent *Mpls./St. Paul* from using the term "Twin Cities" in its logo. It seemed to an outsider's eye a small war on a limited battlefield. "You couldn't come to Minneapolis and live here," Anderson thought, "unless you had people, a family, some roots." I had none of those, but a mind full of cotton, and realized I'd have to leave the city before I was completely destroyed. Jim and I made designs for Boston, suddenly passing over Chicago and St. Louis and Gary, Indiana, and all the places in between in our anxiety to get — we thought — some good fish at the Union Oyster House and a fresh supply for our noses. The flight was nightmarish, much turbulence and disorder and a screeching landing, and although the fish at the Oyster House was wonderful as always, the cocaine was nowhere to be found. We started the long and arduous pain of withdrawal. The high times of Minneapolis abruptly became the grim Edge City of the East.

Coming back East is always homecoming for me, but I am always also out of kilter, out of touch, out of tune with it. Jerry Rosen, in his novel *The Carmen Miranda Memorial Flagpole*, describes the East Coast as the planet Peseema, the place where anything is possible but you *expect* the worst to happen all the time. Nobody tries to live on ideals. Everybody cares about money. The stretch from Washington, D.C., along the coast to Boston is population-packed with cynics and fearful people. It's an exaggerated vision, this Peseema; actually people are happy everywhere on earth when their internal needs are being met, and one can even live in New York City in blissful innocence and optimism, but it's more difficult there. There are more obstacles to be overcome, more *people*. And that's why the place draws me like a magnet, why I can never escape from its clutches; it's littered end to end with people I know and love, great characters, old friends, mother, father, brothers, sister, dozens of aunts and uncles, hundreds of cousins. The East is the greatest, darkest drama of all in our land. We Eastern-ers think we run not only the country, but the world. Seattle natives were always unduly impressed that I'd studied at the great universities of Boston — it was worth many times more to me the farther I got from Boston. Media is focused here, as are industry, money, politics. The politicians are still crooked and every-body knows it and nobody really thinks he can beat it. It's sewn up, you have to be tough to make it, your little bundle of prayers, hopes, talent, or good looks won't get you on the New York subway. Old graveyard of Paul Revere, old hoary haunted stuff, oilcloth kitchens on cold winter mornings in Lawrence, stone fences in Vermont, and the tart wisdom of the Maine coast all flooded my mind. Here, surely, was Yankee industry and savvy, here you had to be on the alert for every change in the weather.

We packed into an old car and drove from Boston along Route 2 west out to the Berkshire hills, stopping in dark Fitchburg to savor outrageous Italian sand-wiches made in a boxcar diner where the Red Sox game dominated the consciousness of all the pale customers.

Burleson was on third, but Yastrzemski couldn't get him over. "They oughta get rid of that fuckin' old Polack," a voice announced to a murmur of agreement in the room, and oh God I was back in Massachusetts and out of coke and surrounded by familiar obligations, a prisoner of my past. We felt we were in the eye of the storm. Jim and I looked at each other longingly and sighed. We alone knew we'd left Minneapolis behind.

We headed out to western Massachusetts and a certain communal farm where I'd lived years ago. One of my main objectives on the trip was to have dinner at the Home Comfort Restaurant in Greenfield, Massachusetts, which was so successful when it opened in 1974 that I couldn't get in for dinner until my third try. It was worth the wait, too. Greenfield, Massachusetts, is a town of 30,000 people that has only recently acquired any idea of itself as sophisticated. It's always been a place for the farm people of neighboring towns to do their shopping and trading and, until Home Comfort, its only dining experiences were conventional lunchroom cafés and a couple of "family restaurants" open to 9 P.M., plus of course the fast-food franchises. Home Comfort was the town's first venture into quiche and curry, the menu changed daily, and while the food was lovingly prepared, customers were plentiful.

The restaurant's founders, Elliot and Katherine Blinder, had lived on several of the area communes before buying their own spread in Charlemont, Massachusetts, "the Yankee Doodle town," and Home Comfort simply adapted the many nourishing and delicious meals we'd kitchen-tested for years in our communal homes. The decor, too, owed a lot to our utopian rural existences — wood everywhere, homeliness of a beautiful and comfortable sort, the feeling of being in some log cabin of a winter's night.

While the operation was new, ideals ran high and enthusiasm was unlimited. The food seemed always exquisite — each day a new challenge to surpass the day before. Reviews of the restaurant appeared all over New England, mostly raves. The Mobil Oil Company taped and aired a nationwide commercial using Home Comfort as an example of virtuous private industry. For several years, it was so crowded on Saturday night that you couldn't get in the door without a reservation and couldn't get a word into Elliot or Katherine's ears. They ran around madly serving the customers until the evening ended in total exhaustion. By Sunday noon, people were lining up at the doors again, demanding lunch. It was never really restful, always demanded more work, sometimes made good profits but in other months lost money on equipment, taxes, mistakes. Even in its most prosperous months, Elliot said, "We damn near went bankrupt three different times."

Meanwhile, providing the diners with all the comforts of home was taking its toll on the quiet home life of the Blinders. They hadn't much time left to enjoy their farm in Charlemont. They had to drive the twenty miles into Greenfield even in the most inclement weather or disappoint a lot of people, employees and customers alike, and pass up a lot of money. By the end of 1976 Elliot and Katherine separated, as young couples will. He moved to the Los Angeles area and began writing scripts, and she was left in charge of the restaurant, the farm, and the two kids.

The decline of the Home Comfort restaurant through 1976 was plain to everybody but apparently irreversible. The publicity of earlier years kept some cutomers coming in, but people stopped making repeat visits. As with many small businesses that rely on the energy of one or two people, the restaurant seemed to die when Katherine became obviously exhausted by its struggles and, in effect, gave up the spirit. The food diminished in quality and the service became superficial. Even the cooks seemed lost in a torpid state. It became no longer difficult to get a table at any time or day, but eating at the Home Comfort by 1977 was like attending a wake. "Too bad she died; she made such lovely doughnuts," as my Irish relatives used to say. The restaurant went quietly under and is no more. It planted the seeds, though, for other good restaurants in the town.

I spoke to Katherine in Greenfield and also to Elliot in L.A. about the restaurant's failure, and both of them seemed more relieved than anguished. It had served its historical purpose, Elliot said; "It kept a bunch of people employed for three years and taught us all a lot of lessons. One of which is that you can't make money in the restaurant business, at least not small restaurants, unless you work like crazy all the time and can wait out the periods when the public gets tired of you and deserts you." Like most businesses that fail, the Home Comfort had lost its heart before it lost its clientele.

Thirty miles north, in Brattleboro, Vermont, another youth-oriented restaurant called The Common Ground has gone in the opposite direction, sailing into its seventh year with larger crowds and better food all the time. The Common Ground has never been the responsibility of any one or two people, but throughout its history it has usually had a couple of dominant egos, overwhelming personalities. It's officially managed and owned by a workers' collective, which, despite a dose of sanctimonious self-sacrifice, appears to be efficient and creative. The restaurant is a second-floor walkup above the hardware store on Eliot Street in the center of Brattleboro. Like Home Comfort was, it's supposed to look like a communal living room in the woods, and it carries that approach to the point of having the diners bus their own dishes. But it's not cheap, about $7 for a meal, not including drinks (beer and wines are offered), in 1977.

I spoke with Fritz Hewitt, who was the manager of the restaurant the day I visited, but who also reverts to being chief dishwasher at times. The thing is organized in one of those tediously democratic fashions wherein nobody is allowed to play chief for too long. Like Bookpeople, The Common Ground sells stock to its employees, who must sell it back when they leave their jobs. And like Bookpeople, it's been favored with employees who are devoted to its cause and work hard more out of a sense of loyalty and faith than for material rewards. Fritz Hewitt is one of the personalities who fire the restaurant's engines; he's also a popular local character around Brattleboro who runs for office now and again and has been called a kind of ambassador between the communes and the natives. Fritz came to Brattleboro in 1968, the same year I arrived with my communal family, but he lived with another group, called the Baby Farm, whose house at Johnson's Pasture burned down the first winter, claiming four lives. Fritz was a Yale dropout, originally from upstate New York, and he had always eschewed the prevalent, bizarre hair styles and clothing styles in favor of a clean-cut, conservative approach that left him presentable enough to talk to the farmers. We did feel, when we first arrived in these woods, that we had to be enormously respectful and polite toward the natives in order to be good neighbors — no matter what strange rituals we practiced at home.

It would be too easy, and too early, to come to the conclusion that the fates of the two restaurants prove that collectively owned companies outdistance those that are owned privately. But it's fair to say that the small business owned by a few people can survive only if their creators remain interested, keep their faith somehow, don't get bored or discouraged. Not every personality is capable, like Mo Siegel, of sustaining the energy for business. The government's Small Business Administration in 1976 reported that 80 percent of small businesses do *not* survive three years. The Common Ground in Brattleboro has made it through countless turnovers in staff because there are enough people in southern Vermont who need a job and believe in the guiding principles of the restaurant to fill the vacancies. It, too, could be the victim of collapse if the youthful idealism ever peters out.

Brattleboro, Vermont, had changed in ten years beyond our wildest expectations. In 1968, it was a sleepy village of 10,000 hardworking Vermonters who paid their bills, drank their liquor, and kept to themselves. There were two movie theatres and a couple of workingmen's bars, no night life. Ours was the first commune to arrive on the scene, and we were regarded at first with some suspicion. A small boy on a Brattleboro street corner tugged his mother's arm and asked, "Mommy, who are those people?" when we walked by, *en masse,* in our overalls and mud-caked boots, long hair and beads. "Oh, those people are *rich,*" she replied. We were rich because we'd come from the city, rich because we bought a hundred-acre farm for $25,000 and we *didn't* farm it, rich because we came to town with money to spend but we didn't *work.* Writing articles and books and commuting to Boston to teach college classes was our income-producing work, but it was invisible to the natives. A party of drunken young men with shotguns came up the mountain one evening to tell us how hard their fathers had worked to scratch a living out of this rocky soil, and who were we to come and make it look so easy?

But we were harbingers, it seems in retrospect, and more communes came, and retirees from city life, and Vermont has been so steadily filling up with newcomers in the last decade that it now has a campaign on to save "the Thurd" — a fictitious cartoon animal who represents the one-third of Vermont's population which is now native-born in the state. It's almost as if the Vermonters think of themselves as a nation. They have their own language and code of honor.

But Brattleboro no longer belongs to Vermonters, if it *is* still in Vermont. The town is now the scene of dozens of new shops, a selection of discos and bars and restaurants catering to a city mentality, a booming countercultural night life, new theatres, a huge record store, new industries. C.E.T.A. money arrived, and an old church was restored to a public arts center, where theatre and readings and lectures are held. You can get a snifter of Courvoisier in a place that plays soft blues music at 1:30 A.M. The Stephen Greene Press and associated bookstore, The Book Cellar, are still on Main Street but the press has prospered (hit sales of $1 million for the first time in 1977) with homey how-to-do-it Vermont lore, and has expanded to new offices and warehouse space. The Book Press, quality book printers and binders, may still be the biggest business and employer in town, but it is no longer the only one. Harry Saxman and Myron Golden of Guilford, city refugees in the eye of the hippie world when they arrived in Vermont, had gone straight enough to establish a carob brokerage, Springtree Corporation, out of Brattleboro offices. They went into carob at precisely the right time, as chocolate increased in price drastically and the major chocolate companies began to use increasing proportions of carob. The raw materials come from Spain by ship to Virginia, where the Saxman-Golden plant produces the carob for United States clients. It's a major natural vegetable substitute for chocolate to the health-food world as well, and its popularity here is still growing. The Marlboro Music Festival draws crowds of city folks in the summer, and the ski resorts in the winter. When we moved to Packer Corners in 1968, we had no neighbors in any direction for two miles, with one exception — a couple to whom we were closely related, who lived separately in a shack down an impossible road. In 1978, every empty house within those two miles was occupied with year-round residents. We found ourselves neighbors to some illustrious writers, professors, and musicians. The value of our property went through the roof. Today it's priceless. We went to Vermont to get away from it all, and saw it all turn into Action Central before our eyes. Brattleboro had turned into a small Aspen or Woodstock.

The farm down in Montague, Massachusetts, where we had edited Liberation News Service in 1968–1969, had transferred its political energy post-Vietnam and post-Watergate to the business of fighting the nuclear power plants. The group in Montague was instrumental in the Seabrook, New Hampshire, demonstrations and arrests, and under its company name of Green Mountain Post Films has turned out a couple of scorching documentaries about nuclear power that make you shake in your boots: *Lovejoy's Nuclear War* and *The Last Resort*. GMP Films is nothing more or less than the same friends gathered around the fire in an old Massachusetts farmhouse, but they have the latest technological equipment and phones, etc., in incongruous harmony with woodstoves and tools of the earth. The first movie, *Lovejoy's Nuclear War*, was shown on public T.V. nationwide and also found some sympathetic theatre bookings in major cities. GMP Films has made a profit on it, according to Dan Keller, the film's director, but all of the money coming in is constantly flowing out into new movies. It's the old familiar story, "that old perplexity the empty purse." Anyway, the film stemmed from communard Sam Lovejoy's bold destruction of a nuclear plant's weather tower in the middle of the night of Washington's Birthday, 1975. The proposed plant, for which the weather tower was constructed, was to be in Montague Plains, just a few miles from where Sam and friends lived on the old L.N.S. farm. Sam himself was also a native of the immediate area and descendant of a family which had literally come over on the *Mayflower*. He turned himself in to the startled Greenfield police the next morning, pleading that he had felled the tower on behalf of all the citizens of Montague and the region — for their protection against the menace and hidden dangers of the nuke. The ensuing trial was sensational, with experts flying in from all parts of the world to testify on the dangers of nuclear energy, but the judge took the easy way out and acquitted Sam on a technicality. Sam had been charged with destroying public property; the weather tower and nuclear power plant were *private* property. The judge was evidently relieved not to have to make a landmark decision on whether or not civil disobedience is proper to defend the people from nuclear power mishaps and horrors of nuclear waste; Sam was predictably pissed off. The GMP cameras had taken the whole drama step by step, and the film that followed was gripping and hair-raising, if more than a little bit amateurish. *The Last Resort* had a more professional quality, and as the company grows, its skills and equipment are refined. So I hung around there and heard all about the scary nuclear stuff. It was funny to think of myself as coming from Washington State, where governor Dixy Lee Ray is perhaps the most fervent nuclear advocate in the land, into this hotbed of organized opposition in the East. We could use these guys out in Seattle, I thought, but they'd be bored to death there after a week. Not enough media input, not enough action.

Jim and I buzzed back down to Boston in some dealer's Rent-a-Car and before he said it I knew that he was returning to the West Coast on the next available plane. I couldn't blame him, either. I had further work to do and relatives to visit, but Jim was along for a good time, and Massachusetts wasn't as much of a good time as California is. We paid a final visit to the Union Oyster House, where Jim astonished the waitress by eating through two lobster dinners and a mountain of clams, plus salad, vegetables, and numerous rounds of drinks. We took a taxi out to Logan Airport and I sent Jim off to San Francisco. He pressed a $100 bill in my hand, saying, "I couldn't leave a friend in a town like this without at least $100." I took the subway back into Boston and sought out David Godine.

David Godine is a Boston publisher, but of a particular and unique sort. The quality of his production work on books is so high that the experienced eye can spot a Godine title on a shelf from across the room. He uses the finest papers, bindings, and creative typefaces to produce a range from $3.95 paperbacks to hand-bound limited editions at great expense. He publishes living authors (Howard Nemerov, Andre Dubus, John Hollander, William Gass), but is also famous for reviving dead books by dead authors (like *The Narrative of Arthur Gordon Pym*, by Edgar Allan Poe, or *Specimen Days* by Walt Whitman). A lot of poetry, natural history, photography, and art. Really elegant books that are a pleasure to hold in your hand, the kind of quality that mass production seems to prohibit these days. Godine's company is small, but his good reputation is pervasive in the book world.

I rounded the Boston Common and Public Garden and plodded up Commonwealth Avenue toward Godine's offices on Dartmouth Street, dreaming of my college daze. The stuff we did, the plain madness we lived out on CommAve makes the goony antics of the movie *Animal House* seem innocent fun. Godine's offices were on the third floor of a restored Back Bay mansion which itself had an academic air. The foyer and staircases were magnificent, the perfect setting, I thought, for the home of Godine's elegant books, but by the time I'd ascended to the top floor and found David sharing an office with two of his editors, I felt I'd entered some garret of the soul. The esthetes lived in this slope-roofed attic, while the moneyed interests lived below. Small rooms were devoted to shipping, billing, receiving, graphic design; a handful of employees seemed bent over their tasks. Godine himself takes the unusual approach of complaining (honestly, I'm sure) that there's no profit to be made in books of such high quality, of lamenting the high price of printing and paper which has forced him to *reduce* the standards he set ten years ago, and characterizing himself as a poverty-stricken artist devoted to the dying art of fine bookmaking. He wrote in the "Publisher's Note" of his Winter 1976 catalogue: "At the end of each year, we look at the depressing figures, shake our heads, issue a few solemn pronouncements about how things will improve and we'd better cut our overhead, and invariably, just as before, get right on with it. With astral regularity, the Spring and Fall lists appear and, with the perverse luck of the innocent, we manage to pull through — usually hanging by our toenails. Why?

"There are lots of answers. Perseverance, ego, stupidity, arrogance. But over the long haul the company continues because we all BELIEVE in what we are doing; and we believe as much in the way we publish as in the books themselves."

It was odd and unexpected to be hearing such tales of poverty from a press that turns out what some people think are the most beautiful books in the country. Godine started in a deserted barn in Brookline in 1969 and is the sole proprietor of the business — "a situation which I don't like but I can't see much point in selling stock in a business that loses money." At the beginning, though, he had two associates and a small bankroll. In 1977, his line of credit was up to $65,000 — but that's very little for the kind of dreams David Godine has. You can see him staring out a window at the Boston skyline and you know he's thinking about parchment from Cambridge, England. Or a certain kind of marbled end papers from Japan.

His particular temptation from the virtuous path of art was an executive post at the Book-of-the-Month Club's Quality Paperback Book Club division. Godine took the job part-time and commuted back and forth from New York to Boston for a year, but finally came back to full-time management of his own small enterprise. "I liked the people at Book-of-the-Month Club, and they wanted me to stay and work full-time, but I couldn't be an editor there because book clubs are not publishing, and the only editorial decisions I had to make involved choosing from books already on the press. If you're bright and you like making decisions, it's hard to give it up: the book clubs just follow a formula." (That reminded me of a manuscript which was submitted to me at Montana Books, called "Book of the Month Club Selection" and allegedly written by the fugitive Yippie, Abbie Hoffman. I had no contact with Abbie himself, but the book had his distinctive sense of humor in it and I believed he was the author, especially as his wife was negotiating for its publication. But Abbie refused to change the title, it was said, and the title of course prevented the book from getting published. No publisher, no matter how small, could afford to suffer the legal ramifications of publishing a book called "Book of the Month Club Selection," unless it existed just to create a Dadaistic sensation and then quickly go out of business.) At any rate, David Godine couldn't say he hadn't had his chance to direct a major media empire.

Something in all of us rebels against the idea of losing money in business; that is, common sense says that if David Godine's been a publisher for ten years that he cannot be "losing money" over that period of time. Businesses which lose money sooner or later have to be bailed out or covered by other money, perhaps a bank's or a private investor's. Some small companies are subsidiaries of large corporations which cover their losses, but nobody, it seems, is willing to invest in a losing thing indefinitely. Godine claims he's been able to hang on by living frugally — on $7,500 a year income after taxes — in Boston. It seemed impossible, but it was true.

Not every innovative business in Boston was in the red. I tried to crack the secretarial barriers at Erewhon Natural Foods, one of the oldest and richest of the natural-foods distributors, which had started with a health-food shop on Newbury Street, but I found the bureaucracy too taxing, the people there never returned my calls and seemed to be too busy to offer me anything but the standard tour of the plant. Erewhon is Nowhere spelled backward, the creation and sole property of Michio Kuchi, a Japanese macrobiotic guru. Its Los Angeles branch was bought by its employees from Michio, but the Boston headquarters still exists to serve his food philosophies. He is also the owner of *East-West Journal*, which addresses itself to the spiritual community and *from* which a new magazine, *New Age Journal*, was formed after a partial staff walkout. Kuchi refused to sell *East-West* to its staff, but he did let *New Age* have his mailing list. I wrote a column for the new magazine, and used it as an office/hangout during my visits to Boston. With a circulation of 30,000 copies after two years, it was still located in a Brookline storefront and still paying its writers a nickel a word. The magazine took a sober approach toward every new religious cult and health idea that came along, but the people who worked there were smokers and drinkers and nonbelievers like myself and we had a good time.

Eric Utne, *New Age*'s publisher, showed me figures which seemed to indicate that the magazine was turning a small profit, but that was his mistake as I then began agitating for more than a nickel a word. Writers should not be paid by the word anyway; it encourages them to be long-winded and unnecessarily verbose. Since many of the articles were written by adherents of various religious outfits and sensitivity groups, the authors went on at interminable lengths and the editors had to balance their need to cut the copy with the hyper-sensitivity of their writers. Eric was the publisher of the magazine, his wife, Peggy, the editor, and his brother Tom the production man. You had to like the Utnes to like the magazine, but I did; they were terribly earnest intellectuals but always vulnerable to a good laugh at the expense of the guru-kissers. I saw my own function at the magazine as being one of ridiculing the readers for the benefit of the underpaid, overworked editors.

Eric and Peggy separated in 1978, and she went on publishing *New Age* while he hooked up with Bob Schwartz's Executive Conference Center at Tarrytown, New York. Bob Schwartz is a multimillionaire entrepreneur who's a leading theoretician of the new spiritual subcultures. His mission is to convince the disaffected young that American business needs them and will give them room to be themselves; he bridges the extremes of Esalen, est, and humanistic psychology versus banking, business, and money. He insists that money itself is not the goal of the new entrepreneurs, but only a "lubricant" for social change. His economic mentor is E. F. Schumacher, whose book *Small Is Beautiful* has permeated the subculture. The old idea that "Bigger is Better" is out now, we are told, but Schwartz himself has been associated with some of the largest corporations in the country. The old power structure meets the new, but power is still the name of the game.

I went home to enjoy the enclosure of my parents' home, my brother's and sister's homes, little nieces and nephews, hot meals and clean socks and old photographs and tales, all the things that come with being the son of a large Massachusetts enclave of Irish and French-Canadians, families who stick together despite anything, work hard, drink hard at times, still go to church and pray for the dead, and follow the Red Sox. My uncle Jean-Paul still insists that the Red Sox bet against themselves with the local Boston bookies just in the heat of the pennant races and deliberately take a dive just to make money. Uncle has no proof but he's been saying it for thirty years because the people of New England are conditioned to believe that everything and everybody that *could* be crooked, probably *is*. They've had so many scandals over the years that they naturally wait for the next one. *Scandal* and *tragedy* are two words that are wildly overused in Boston — there's always one or the other in the news.

When Tony Conigliaro, the Red Sox outfielder, got beaned and had to retire from baseball, it was "tragedy." Now Tony C. does a sports show in San Francisco, but he still lives and dies for the Red Sox, who are more of a religious devotion than a mere ballclub to the natives. I myself was attracted to the shrine, Fenway Park, and spent every available afternoon or evening out there smoking joints which were passed down the rows in the bleachers, screaming for the Red Sox, secretly loathing them in my heart, secretly knowing that they'd find a way to lose in the end — preferably the very end.

I headed north again, this time to check out my brother's little movie theatre in Newburyport, Massachusetts, and on to New Hampshire and Maine. Newburyport proved to be a sweet and restful town, a beach resort without most of the crap that goes with it, preciously restored colonial buildings and a conservative and honest-Yankee attitude. My brother Andrew and his partner, Nancy Langsam, had started a tiny theatre operation called the Newburyport Screening Room, which was open on weekends and moved itself all over town to various rented halls, the Y.M.C.A., etc. Newburyport did not have a movie theatre in the village itself before they started the Screening Room, but there is a modern twin-cinema a few miles out of town on the highway. The movie operation was very small and personal, hugely appreciated by its patrons, and has now grown into a permanent location; there's not anymore to say about it except to note that I spent hours hauling around the portable theatre, screen, projectors, speakers, folding canvas chairs, posters, etc., there was no real profit in it, but we had hopes, and I felt once again that old remorse about business: about how hard it really is when you're starting out, and how distant the rewards seem. It takes a lot of heart and an incredible tolerance and patience to stick it out.

Portsmouth, New Hampshire, passed in a blur. Ten years ago it had decrepit waterfront neighborhoods that have since been restored and spruced-up and made into Colonial Heritage Tourist Time. Same story all over the coasts, it seemed to me. The waterfront restorations are sometimes beautiful, but they drive out families and ethnic neighborhoods and derelicts in favor of white folks with money to spend. I was privileged to borrow the use of a new waterfront apartment in Boston, which had provided for families of different income groups to occupy the same building—so that welfare mothers and successful executives rode up and down the elevators together; but for the most part, that level of concern and social thoughtfulness is still rare in this country. I found some old friends in Portsmouth saddened by the disappearance of their son, who'd had an automobile accident which may have impaired his memory, was seen running from his battered truck, and hadn't been heard from in over two years. He was presumed either dead or amnesiac. Great military aircraft went up and down with ear-piercing sonic booms, and in nearby Seabrook thousands of demonstrators were being arrested for blocking the grounds of a proposed nuclear power plant. New Hampshire's state motto is "Live

Free or Die," and it wasn't clear which would win out in the end.

Up in Kennebunk, Maine, calm was restored. Maine is already so doomed by her physical remoteness and numbing cold winter that one can't feel any strong concern about political catastrophes when one is there. Maine exists in an ice-locked dream, and although I was there in August, already the first cold winds were blowing and the streets of Kennebunk were quiet and empty. I searched for an hour for a company called Tom's Natural Soaps, which has saturated the health market with natural soaps, shampoos, and toothpastes all bearing sunny, friendly messages from "your friend, Tom." The company employs slick magazine advertisements featuring the proprietor's cute children using Tom's products in the bathroom in their little 'jammies. I smelled another Celestial Seasonings, but actually I was wrong. The first problem I had to face was finding the factory on Railroad Avenue, when the only Railroad Avenue I could find was a dirt path and the only building on it was called the Kennebunk Chemical Center. Which turned out, of course, to be the parent company of Tom's Natural Soaps.

Tom Chappell is a Massachusetts native who graduated from Trinity College in Hartford, Connecticut, in 1966 and was working as an insurance company salesman when he and his wife decided to move to Maine from Philadelphia in search of a better environment in which to raise their kids. His father manufactures pollution abatement products, chemicals that you add to polluted waters to help clear them up. Tom decided to go into pollution preventions rather than cures, and in August 1970 began making phosphate-free detergents under the trade name ClearLake. These detergents were not "natural" products, but were less polluting than ordinary detergents, and the Kennebunk Chemical Center still produces them, but the "natural" end of the business has surpassed it in sales. Tom's first natural soaps came out in 1972, to be followed by the shampoos and toothpaste and, now at last, deodorants. There is *some* small percentage of detergent in Tom's shampoos but the dominant ingredients are "edible" in their original forms — things like apple cider vinegar, glycerine drawn from vegetable sources, herbs and oils. Only Dr. Bronner's famous peppermint-oil soap is equally pure, but Dr. Bronner has organized the business as a church and the soap comes in a bottle that is covered with Christ-consciousness philosophies all strung together in a row without periods or commas like this. Tom's marketing approach is slick, neat, aimed at middle America. It's working, too. "Sales have nearly doubled every year since 1970," Tom says. "The average rate of growth is about 80 percent per year, and at present (1979) sales are in the millions."

But it's still Kennebunk, Maine, in an old railroad warehouse and the payroll of about thirty people is still a small enough group to be close. The soap is made in old dairy storage tanks. The employees have their own names on the coffee cups. The enterprise didn't seem to have the frantic and earth-shaking energy of a Celestial Seasonings, and nobody could think Kennebunk is another Boulder. The pace was relaxed.

Dick Pickering, who was a high-school English teacher in Kennebunk before joining Tom as distribution manager assigned to the western states, took me on the grand tour of the plant. "What is real and good will find its place and endure," he said, in reference to Tom's products. He was obviously happy with their success, most people there seemed pretty happy, too; I couldn't help feeling glad for them. Business is great, the world is coming to their door, they believe in what they're doing, and they don't have to leave Maine. I drove off with free samples of spearmint and fennel toothpaste and a tube of Tom's shaving cream. The shaving cream simply didn't make the big lather that regular shaving creams do, and I never found it satisfactory preparation for cutting my beard. The fennel toothpaste had a strong licorice taste, which my kids liked, but I preferred the spearmint, which was delicious. Actually, I know from my three years as a "complete restorative patient" at the University of Washington's Dental School that toothpaste is almost completely worthless for fighting tooth decay anyway. It's not the sugar you eat that makes cavities, but the interaction of the sugar with your plaque, and that plaque can be brushed away as well with or *without* toothpaste. Some toothpaste has fluoride, which is beneficial, but only in tiny traces. You get more fluoride in some drinking water, and in nature. Toothpaste "sweetens your breath" for sure, but the student dentists claimed that no mouth deodorant is effective for much more than 20 minutes. Finally, toothpaste is for the most part a cosmetic nicety, it really doesn't help much in providing good dental health, it's the brushing and flossing that counts. My dentists knew all this and were quite casual about telling me so, but I was *astounded* by the information. Toothpaste is, after all, an absolute necessity for most of us, and that because we've been told over and over that if we don't use it we'll get cavities and have to go to the dentist and be in PAIN. Fear of his buzzing drills and evil little scalpels makes for a powerful selling point. So if you have to have toothpaste, Tom's spearmint tastes great.

I had a final appointment in Maine with John Cole, then the editor of *The Maine Times* in Topsham, an eleven-year-old weekly newspaper with a 25,000 circulation which is an excellent representative of "the new weeklies." You know what I mean. While daily newspapers have been in decline for decades and T.V. has taken over a large part of the news market, the underground press of the 1960s paved the road for the community weekly papers of the 1970s, many of which are prosperous. They usually offer a liberal or progressive point of view but they are not outrageous, obscene, or radical. They are "attractively designed," to use a seventies expression, usually a tabloid format with full-page photograph on the cover, sharp, clean typefaces and restrained graphics. People use them as a handy guide to movies, T.V., galleries, music and theatre events, sports; they also review restaurants. And around all those utilitarian items there's usually room for a special point of view, a little good writing. The weeklies of the seventies, history may say, existed not to foment social change so much as to cast a slightly jaundiced eye on it.

The grandparent of the form is New York's *Village Voice*, which has evolved all the way from its bohemian roots to joining the sensationalistic-journalism empire of the Australian publishing baron, Rupert Murdoch. Boston has *The Phoenix* and *The Real Paper*, Denver the *Straight Creek Journal*, San Francisco the *Bay Guardian*, Seattle the *Weekly* and the *Sun*. The whole lot of them held a convention in Seattle that was written up by Calvin Trillin in *The New Yorker* as a real yawner; they were more interested in discussing advertising rates than hot social issues.

Now *The Maine Times* is atypical of its form in some important respects. Unlike the other weeklies, it doesn't relate to a metropolitan area but to an entire state, and is published out of a small coastal village. It also projects the state of Maine far beyond its borders to Maine-lovers all over the world; I've been reading it in recent months off the coffee table of a friend in Carmel, California. It relates as much to rural survival skills as to arts, cuisine, or town life. And, while nobody would call it wild or radical (except perhaps the extreme right), it has consistently taken a civil-libertarian point of view and offered a progressive opinion on state and national affairs. Most of that point of view, and some of the paper's most ethereally beautiful writing, had come from John Cole. Listen to this:

> Here in Maine, the cold is elemental and absolute;
> even the sea has been congealed. Snows can still

isolate and immobilize; fires must be built and care taken, otherwise we shall freeze. None of us can make light of the cold; its intensity is awesome and purifying. There is in its cleanliness a kind of religious dedication. By its very persistence the cold seeks to convert us to an acknowledgment of nature's might. (Cole in *The Boston Globe.*)

Or this:

But the grapes are on the vine, and as I make daily, discreet checks on their progress I can see visions of my demise as a gardening ignoramus. There is something about the small green spheres and the knowledge of what they can become that tempts me to discard my finely wrought image as a botanical boob and take up hoe, rake and pruning shear with all the vigor I have known all along I could muster.

It is wine, of course, which lures me to squander the years invested in proclaiming seedling stupidity; I am prepared to gamble a decade of professed, and now credible, agricultural dumbness because I am finally convinced that wine does, indeed, come from grapes. (From *The Maine Times.*)

It took me about a half-hour to find the newspaper's office once I was in Topsham, and that was amazing because the entire commercial part of town wasn't more than two blocks long. "Blink and you'll miss it," John Cole had said on the phone. I must have passed it three or four times before I found the old Victorian house that had been transformed into *The Maine Times* and other businesses. Cole met me at the door and we walked through the layout rooms and offices up to his office on the second floor, which was rich in books, art, and trophies. Cole is in his mid-fifties, married with six children, graduated from Yale in '45, was a combat gunner in the war, then a New York public relations man, then spent seven years as a commercial fisherman (some of them with Peter Matthiessen) on Long Island. He came to Maine in 1958 and is most widely known for his work in conservation and articles in magazines. He does some teaching (journalism classes) at Bowdoin College and has won many awards and distinctions. But knowing all of that about him doesn't prepare you for the real person he is, for the salty wit and booming voice and his tremendous, earth-shaking laughter. He put his feet on the desk and told me the story of *The Maine Times*. The trees outside his windows had begun to turn although it was only late August, and the first winds of winter bent them and blew them in a silent ballet.

As we spoke, John Cole had, after ten years, just sold most of his stock in the newspaper and "retired" from editing it to work on a book (about striped bass), write editorials and his column, go to auctions, and generally carry on his environmental research. I asked him if he was sorry to step down from his role of managing the newspaper and he roared, "Hell no! I worked like a horse on the thing and I'm glad it's on its feet and glad as hell to get some money out of it. I'm relieved. And I'm free!" He added, "The best thing about being a writer is that they can't hand you some goddamn watch and tell you you're through. As long as somebody out there is willing to pay me and publish my stuff, I can go on doing it until I die. Writing's the best racket of all."

And John Cole is some kind of writer's dream of a newspaper editor, irreverent and gruff but good-humored, intelligent, inflamed with the spirit to fight the good causes to the end. Here is a guy, I thought, who obviously enjoys what he does. And so I enjoyed sitting around shooting the bull with him until dark shadows of night closed in on us.

I drove back to Boston on the toll road, the only fast route, silently cursing as periodic toll plazas lightened my purse. Only in the eastern third of the country do we have toll highways, and after years of driving on western "freeways," I'd forgotten how the people have to pay and pay on the Atlantic coast, and you wonder where the money goes because the roads aren't even necessarily in good repair. I visited Marty Linsky, editor of *The Real Paper*, at its bustling Cambridge offices on the middle floors of a new high-rise building. The paper had come a long way since its inception as a protest against the direction *The Phoenix* was taking. The original *Real Paper* editors were former *Phoenix* editors who'd walked out. I forget what the issue was, but it's dead now anyway. *The Phoenix* continues more as a weekly guide to the arts around Boston — movie listings, record reviews, etc. — while *The Real Paper* takes a more consciously political view of life in the city and has, in my opinion, a higher standard of writing. If its views are left of center, its corporate structure is ordinary enough, and it plainly exists to make money for its stockholders, who include David Rockefeller *fils*, son of the banker. "It started out funky but it's a serious business now," Linsky said.

The strains and tensions of deadlines and information input were everywhere in the air. The phones rang, people ran around, the place buzzed and everybody talked fast. I retreated to my parents' simple kitchen, glad that blood is thicker than water.

I knew I had to leave Boston when the Red Sox lost thirteen out of fourteen games and slipped from their well-fortified first-place position. Tragedy. My vision began to blur. I couldn't tell one hip entrepreneur from another. But I was broke and so sat in the *New Age* office hoping for a miracle, which transpired in the person of a pleasant woman editor who invited me out for a drink and, hearing my plight, cheerfully loaned me $200 from her purse. It was almost enough to fly to Seattle, but for some reason I thought it would be better to fly to New Orleans, have some cash left over, and trust to my fate and friends in New Orleans to get me out of there. I took off as fast as I could. Fair New England, we'll meet again when the New Age is fizzled out.

You smell the South almost before you see it. The air in New Orleans was heavy with the perfume of late summer flowers; it was hot and slow, stunned by the sun, half-asleep all day and wide-awake in the cool Amaretto evenings. It was the best possible foil to the heavy industry of the Northeast, and I spent the first twenty-four hours sinking into my traditional New Orleans stupor. My friends Steve and Judy Diamond escorted me to their gabled old manse, partially air-conditioned, which also served as the local headquarters of the anti–nuclear power movement in the area. But there were no demonstrations, few phone calls and visitors — in the torpor of the season's weather, few people could bother themselves worrying about nuclear power plants. It was fun to stroll out with them to the all-night music spots after midnight, where I drank Black Russians and smoked big cigars of that brown dope they get down there, moved with all the wasted people of that lowest-down-the-river city.

The Diamonds had a new baby daughter, Crescent, whom we all enjoyed. I fell in love with a dark stranger who looked through me with sad brown eyes. The music played on into the dawn, when the relentless heat came back and we ran for cover. Steve introduced me to the people at the Whole Food Company, Inc., a wonderfully mellow and profitable crew, and I heard their story from Jon Maxwell. It's a retail grocery which tries to sell "good groceries" rather than "health foods" and has reached sales of $450,000 a year with a profit of $25,000 and wages of $4 an hour. The workers all own stock, which they can sell back at a profit and can also keep half of it when they leave. Everybody makes the same four bucks an hour, no matter what kind of work he or she does. Their median age is twenty-five.

And, best of all, these gentle people were trusting enough to let me cash a check for homeward fare even though they realized it wouldn't be a good one for two weeks or so. And when it wasn't even good then, despite my best computation, Steve covered it with funds we'd pioneered out of a New York publisher for Steve's last book. The impressive thing was the complete lack of worry on the Whole Food Company's part; they were used to waiting on payment for checks from friends, and just put it aside with a smile. People with that innocent attitude can scarcely get burned; a decent person bends over backward to pay debts of honor like that. Debts between friends have killed many a good friendship.

But Steve Diamond is more than a friend to me, we lived together on the farms way back when and have had a common purse as long as we can remember. My friends form a second family for me; they're scattered far and wide but they know my house is their own, and when I visit them I feel free to raid the icebox. I don't want to live with my friends, but they are a supportive network and I couldn't live without them. I feel most whole when my kids are living with me and friends are around for a drink. I fled home to Seattle for all of those familiar comforts, but after all the tripping to far places and other people's scenes, I found myself restless and miserable. Nine months passed while I raised my kids, wrestled with early drafts of this book, stared off into space, met the increasingly complex and tedious demands of my bookstore empire, wondered what the hell was the point of business and money, struggled to adapt to my new life as a divorced man, sank into personal bankruptcy, and drank myself into a stupor every night. Couldn't stand it another minute by mid-1978 and hit the road thinking, "Jesus, Mary, and Joseph, I'm a thirty-two-year-old man with kids and a business and I'm out here wondering where to go, I've got no home and I don't give a damn." I sold my last house in Seattle and packed the car with everything it would hold — mostly sentimental value. Sold the nuptial waterbed. And the oak sideboard from the mad blind widow's house. The couch and chairs were simply left behind, the stereo, T.V., and writing desk left with friends. The black night swallowed me. Now I am once again floating in the world, a liquid asset in my own blood and bone.

# 5
# Charity Begins at Home

*"I began to meditate upon the writer's life. It is full of tribulation. First he must endure poverty and the world's indifference; then, having achieved a measure of success, he must submit with a good grace to its hazards. He depends upon a fickle public. . . . But he has one compensation. Whenever he has anything on his mind, whether it be a harassing reflection, grief at the death of a friend, unrequited love, wounded pride, anger at the treachery of someone to whom he has shown kindness, in short any emotion or any perplexing thought, he has only to put it down in black and white, using it as the theme of a story or the decoration of an essay, to forget all about it. He is the only free man."*

—W. Somerset Maugham

Home sweet home(s). When my then-wife and I first came to Seattle, and found the house rental market tighter than skin, we quickly deduced that it might be easier and cheaper to *buy* a house than to rent one. The fact that we had no savings, were living off my sporadic royalties and various forms of public assistance, and were not even legally married yet didn't dissuade us. Seattle was full of empty houses for sale, and we correctly guessed that if we offered to rent (lease) a house for a year with the option to buy it, we could have our choice. Buyers were scarce, and the owner could at least get rent from us while keeping the house actively for sale. We steered clear of the Rental Guide scams and stopped chasing hot ads in the newspaper. We took a grand tour of empty houses in our neighborhood, the Wallingford district, picked out the one we wanted, and got in touch with the landlord. Perfect! It was owned by a developer in the suburbs who was too busy to deal with it for a year anyway.

It was a tidy green double-story house with a wrought-iron eagle mounted under a dormer window which looked on shimmering Lake Union with the downtown skyline in the background. The living room, also, had the supernatural view. Three bdrms., fireplace, w/w carpet, new fixt., sm. yard. The nicest place I'd ever lived, I thought at the time, the perfect place to bring the baby home to. We had no furniture and sat on the w/w carpeting to eat, talk, read. We acquired beds on the last gasp of an expiring credit card, and I raced across the country in a car, picked up her furniture from its storage on Long Island, New York, and raced madly back towing a trailer full of rocking chairs and butcher-block tables and an antique sewing machine.

We paid $175 a month, very steep rent for that part of Seattle in 1973, but we decided to make them an offer they couldn't refuse and named the price ourselves. And so we started our venture into Home Empire, probably still the greatest single investment most people make. The green house was small, a dollhouse with sloped roofs in the upstairs bedrooms and no yard for the kids to play in, and in the spring of seventy-four we decided to buy a house in earnest but not to buy that particular one. Once the owners learned that we weren't going to exercise our option, they began sending prospective buyers over to inspect the place, which led to some fierce and hilarious battles between my wife and the suburban developers, culminating in their being forced to put us all up at a motel *with* room service.

We found the blue house through an ad in the paper. The owners were a newly graduated dentist, his wife, and their two kids, and they were already committed to a grand new condominium in the suburbs and a partnership in a thriving dental practice in one of those new "professional plazas." In view of their affluent future, they seemed to regard the old Seattle house as something of a burden. The market was sluggish in sales, hot in rentals, but they didn't want the *bother* of renting it out. It was a fantastic house, twice the size of the green job, huge dormers and outer rooms, the same great view of Lake Union from another angle, a big green yard and fruit trees, leaded-glass windows, natural hardwood floors and doorways and posts. We bought the thing for a sale price of $19,500 with *no* down payment, closing costs of about $500, and a mortgage payment of $150 a month at 9 percent interest over twenty years. In short, Mr. and Mrs. Dentist got no cash out of selling the house, just $150 a

month (of which they paid their own mortgage payment on the house of $118), leaving them a monthly
income of $32 on the place. In twenty years, we'd have
to cash them out; by that time, their own mortgage
would be paid. They were deliberately postponing all
the goodies for years in order to earn more interest. My
own style is to take the money and run to Venezuela.
Anyway, we ended up *owning* this wonderful house
and our "rent" was *reduced* $25 a month! I thought of
Seattle, "This place is great. They give you exactly
what you need." From the dentist's point of view, too,
it was exactly what he was looking for: a just-the-
right-size nice family that would keep the place stable
and solvent. We didn't tell the dentist that we weren't
yet married (planning to . . . ) because that would have
alarmed his mental computer. We did it as Mr. and
Mrs. and that house became the physical monument of
our union, the family home, as the divorce courts later
called it. We plunged into its restoration. I hate
physical work, but found myself on a high ladder
painting the great house bluer than blue; we wallpa-
pered the living and dining rooms in brilliant floral
designs, a really outrageous print we had to order from
San Francisco, in long, tense weekends that took
advantage of the lower rental rates for the paperhang-
ing kit. We painted every interior wall and ceiling, and
stained the hardwood floors. We made it a palace
acceptable even to my mother. We ate barbecues in the
backyard just like Mr. and Mrs. America and had a big
garden; I had a fantastic marijuana crop the first
summer of Big Blue, but in the second season a

predawn thief made off with my plants, and I realized I couldn't plant my favorite weed there anymore. Despite all this domestic beauty, though, we decided to separate our marital unit and so wound up buying another house around the corner, Minnie Skinner's place.

Now, Minnie's place was like the haunted house of your childhood neighborhood. Minnie herself had spent forty years there going gradually blind and stringing nylon stocking ropes all over the place at shoulder height to guide herself around the rooms. She hadn't moved anything out of the house in years, and every closet was crammed with old newspapers and dusty remembrances of her widow's life. There were three bedrooms upstairs and down and a one-bedroom apartment with private entrance and bath attached to the back of this creaky relic — also a backyard, roses, an old leaky-roof garage and driveway, and a mad neighbor lady who paraded up and down the street in a muumuu. Minnie's heirs consisted of the proverbial distant nephew who turned the house over to lawyers to sell it. I went to the agents as a married man who wanted it for investment and rental income — a respectably ambitious program — when in fact I intended to live in it to commence my new life as a single man. But I never let disconcerting information get in the way of a real estate deal.

The price was only $17,500, with a $3,500 down payment deferred six months and a mortgage payment of $150 less the $100 the back apartment brought in, so a monthly obligation to me of $50! In 1975. The mortgage called for a cash-out within five years; meaning I'd have to refinance it or sell it within that time in order to complete payments to Minnie's estate — "cash it out." It was unbelievably cheap. But you get what you pay for, as the saying goes, and I got the most massive home-repair job of my life, a leaky roof that dripped on my Japanese grass wallpaper, a faulty plumbing system, an expensive furnace, and a great big haunted crazy house to walk around in, single and lonely, hearing the sound of my own voice echoing or sighing over the children's toys scattered about. I also experienced a dearth of sexual activity in Minnie's house; it seemed that whenever I seduced a potential lover to the house with great effort, the deal fell through once we were within its walls. Within six months, I sold it for $5,000 more than I'd paid and moved into a one-bedroom basement apartment at $95 a month, which had been previously occupied by the family to whom I sold the house.

The basement apartment was possibly the least stressful environment I found in Seattle. It was part of the house of an elderly lady who loved children and never invaded my privacy. The $95 included heat and utilities, so there were no bills. When the kids came, they used the bedroom while I slept on the couch in the living room and it wasn't much but it was easy and required no work and I was happy. Lovers came, too. But my ex-wife and I finally sold Big Blue for $38,000, exactly twice what we'd paid a few years earlier, and after taxes and liens and debts, we were left with about $5,000 each from the proceeds of the sale. I knew the I.R.S. would tax me on the income, so I bought another house with my $5,000, sure that I'd otherwise piss it away. I had sold Minnie's house on the same basis on which we bought Big Blue: that is, on a private real estate contract which gave me no cash immediately but seemed to assure a solvent future. I bought a crazy little house on Sloop Place in another part of Seattle, the Ballard neighborhood, and began throwing outrageous Sloop Place Soirées. The people to whom I sold Minnie Skinner's house *also* encountered her ghost and sold it for $40,000. Today, three years later, it's worth maybe $75-85,000, but I doubt that Minnie's spirit has departed.

Sloop Place was one of two tiny streets (the other was called Canoe Place) bordering a pocket park in Seattle's heavily Scandinavian Ballard district. Ballard was once a town of its own, and predated Seattle itself; it was a neighborhood full of real-food shops, butchers and bakeries (real Danish pastry with custard), and greengrocers and fish markets. Churches by the dozen and neatly kept lawns and backyards of Norwegians and Swedes. The three-bedroom house looked into the park and playground across the street, perfect for my kids, who could play in the park and still be in sight. It had w/w shag carpeting so thick and comfortable that guests of my *soirées* more than once ended up sleeping the night out on my living room floor. I never found a quieter or more peaceful house anywhere, even in the remotest wilderness. There were only four houses on Sloop Place and virtually no traffic, although it was only a few blocks off a main artery and within walking distance of shops and buses. It was not, in fact, safe from the stress and anxiety of the city — which for me included my howling creditors and vicious divorce proceedings, which kept an army of shrinks, judges, lawyers, and social workers busy and overpaid. Somebody should figure out just how much money is spent in the divorce business these days; it might even surpass oil and petroleum products. I buried my sorrows on Sloop Place in a river of alcohol, a mountain of dope. The *soirées* became a weekly salon of writers, artists and bookpeople in the city, and the soul-searching talk didn't end till dawn Monday morning. The whole idea of the Sunday night *soirée*, in fact, was to abolish Mondays. The nation would have many fewer ulcers if people had the good sense not to get out of bed on Mondays.

The Sloop Place house cost me $25,000: $5,000 down and $180 a month at 9 percent interest with a five-year cash-out. It was getting more expensive to live in Seattle by 1976, and houses requiring "no money down" had simply disappeared. Simultaneously, the divorce plus unpaid bills were driving me into bankruptcy and I found I couldn't even make the $180 payments on time.

I fled the city for the country house in Index, installing a tenant/housesitter at Sloop Place to share the mortgage cost and keep the place occupied and alive — also to prevent me from having to move my books and furniture and to assuage my feelings of remorse about giving the place up only six months after I'd moved in. It seemed to me I'd been doing a lot of moving, more or less once a year, and I longed for some stability, a place to settle in, and made the mistake over and over of thinking that a physical structure itself, a house, which equals a bundle of money invested, could do the trick. I forgot, in the cauldron of my thirtieth year, that I'd been more settled and content while living in the open air of the mountains of Nepal. The Index scenery, magnificent snow-capped peaks, reminded me of Nepal, but the mere distance from the city didn't quiet my heart. I took the house as a rental at $250 a month and was shortly behind in those payments, too. Nonetheless, the owner, who was a well-known Seattle media personality, deeded me the place before I'd paid him the $7,500 down payment we'd orally agreed upon, and I found myself owning *two* houses and able to pay for neither.

That situation was unsupportable, but it continued on for six months while I got more hopelessly mired in debt, depression, and inertia. I reached the point of not being able to have gas, electric, or telephone service in my own name since I owed money to all of the utilities. And suddenly, in 1977, I sold the Sloop Place house, again on a private-contract basis, to pay some debts and the months of back mortgage owed on it, and simultaneously quit-claimed the Index house back to its owner and fled that town in the night. I went overnight from owning two houses to having none, and lived for a month and a half on a friend's couch, my books and belongings packed up in boxes left in other people's garages and cellars all over Seattle. It looked like the end for me until I met the mad deacon.

The demented deacon walked into the bookstore looking for Aramaic titles, and when our eyes met we both knew we'd met our match. He had an incredible little house in the north end of town with sloping floors, old tiles, a great fireplace, and a big backyard with a fishpond. Garage and second floor playroom for kids. On a major street, so noisy, but it was an unadulterated 1930s Seattle house, very solid, with all its old doorknobs, tiles, frosted glass doors, and built-in shelves and dressers intact, and I always went for that old stuff. To my mind's eye such a house, a Depression-era bungalow, is more beautiful than any modern split-level solar palace of the suburbs. Anyway the *mad* thing about the house, in addition to all its weird quirks and cubbyholes and tiny hallways, was that the deacon had left it empty and unrented for the better part of a year! The deacon owned many houses, and a number of them were always empty; he never advertised them in the newspaper but just waited for the person with the right vibrations to come along. He liked having empty houses, it made him feel secure. He was about my age, early thirties, but with the long black beard and tall black hat and his soberly psyche-delic mien, he seemed like an ancient of the soul. I went to his house, which was a grand one made dark by curtains and shades on all the windows — a great hoary library of religious books, and a flock of impeccably well-behaved children who peered from their bedrooms but didn't enter the living room while he and I were negotiating over the house. I was to pay $250 a month, which would apply toward an eventual down payment of $5,000 on a sale price of $37,000. He had no keys to the place; it didn't lock anyway and you could get in through the garage door. I went there and found the heat on, the electricity functioning, the refrigerator cold and clean, the lawn mower well oiled, the whole scene just sitting there for months waiting to be occupied. Madness. But the deacon was a clear answer to my prayers, and we sealed our bargain with only a handshake and a stare. "Mungo, I like you," he intoned. "Deacon . . . I like your house!" I replied. At $37,000 it was the cheapest house left in Seattle in 1977, when good ones were well into six figures and bad ones at 50-60.

I soon found out why. The house itself was solid and comforting, but it *tilted*. It tilted so much that my kids got into the game of rolling a marble from the dining room and shrieking with glee as it picked up steam in the foyer and living room and finally shot out the front door at fifty miles per hour. There were times when I thought it was actually sinking into the earth. The other problem was the street noise; the house had been built at a time when Eightieth Street was quiet and residential, but today it's a main avenue for big diesel trucks crossing town and sometimes the rumble from the street — ten feet from the front door of the house — made the windows shake.

Only *I* would be mad enough to live here, I thought, but it was a good house for writing in, and the kids liked it and I was grateful for the roof over my head, period. We staged a fine Thanksgiving and Christmas in it, then January came with its inevitable slump in bookstore business and personal enterprise, and I found myself unable to make payments on the house on time, then at all. I was entering the last stages of house-madness and knew I'd seen the movie before, on Sloop Place and in Index: the terrible movie of rent-owing. And the demented deacon, unlike other land-lords and mortgage-holders I'd known, took a late payment as a personal insult. He came steaming up to the house like an elephant in heat at midnight, at dawn, any time of day or night except the Sabbath, to pound on the bedroom window shouting "Ray! Ray! I've got to have my rent! I've got to make my deposit!" Many a midnight I let him in, though I was already well advanced into my nocturnal stupor, and listened to his ancient wails, his cry in the wilderness. "Where's the money?" "I don't have it yet." "Can't you get it from the bookstore?" "Bookstore doesn't have it, either; we're two thousand overdrawn at the bank." "Can't you borrow it from a friend?" "My friends don't have money!" It was bizarre, I was living in fear that this mad philosopher would arrive at any moment, even if I had guests, and burst into his life's complaint. As a friend had said when I told him about the deacon, "He'll *really* be demented when he gets through with you." The same friend had suggested I end my financial despair by changing my name from Mungo to Pro Buono. The deacon and I always ended our conversations on a spiritual note; as soon as he was convinced that I really didn't have the rent, wasn't hiding it under some mattress, he'd turn the conversation to God, and we'd pray together.

Fortunately my prayers were answered a second time when a family I knew, the Freedmans, hit town needing a house. The Freedmans were the same family to whom I had sold Minnie Skinner's house, and they were so spooked by the time *they* sold it that they'd bought a new car, tossed the kids and the family mementos into it, and hightailed it back to Surf City, New Jersey, from which they'd first come to Seattle. They learned a winter's lesson that you can't go back and expect to be content living in New Jersey after you've spent some years in Seattle, if for no other reason than it's too cold there. It might seem a bit of a dirty trick for me to put the Freedmans under the watchful eye of the demented deacon, but the Freedmans were never the kind of people who'd miss a mortgage payment, so I figured the deacon would like them, and he did. One day he came to harangue me as usual and found, instead of me and my furniture, a family of four just arrived from New Jersey with boxes full of clothes and *no* furniture. He was predictably unflustered, and offered to sell the house to the Freedmans on the spot. I had in the meantime moved back to Ballard — on the Sabbath — and taken over a ramshackle house recently vacated by a commune of learning-impaired persons. They had clogged up the wood-burning stove, which was the only source of heat in this hillbilly house, with pop-tops from beer cans. The place was gigantic, and I thought of having another tenant but decided against it, as I had fallen in love with my Sloop Place tenant, and the one thing employers shouldn't do is to fall in love with their employees, or landlords with their tenants. It's just plain bad for business. But I could only rent or share a house of mine with somebody I found intellectually admirable and sexually attractive. It couldn't work, and it didn't.

The Freedmans found out about the tilt and the noise. They bought another house instead of the deacon's but after a month and a half of wrangling with paperwork, the deal fell through. Except for the strange personal kind of house deals I specialized in, house deals are extremely vulnerable to collapse at many points along the way from earnest money to title transference.

Simultaneously, the owner of the hillbilly house, which had a rural mailbox and was on a street with dirt sidewalks, decided to sell it and the Freedmans bought it, marking the third time in two years that they had followed me into a house, and I had to move again after only two months in the latest haven. That was the move that destroyed my last grasping for a physical home; I simply packed the car and took off down the road. For the past six months, I have not lived anywhere. Now all these real estate stories may seem to have no connection to business and money except the business of housing itself. For my purposes, they serve to illustrate one aspect of another business, the business of being a writer, the business of literature.

I'm not saying, of course, that all writers engage in house horse-trading and move around the world like homeless wretches, only that I do, and that may be my particular obsession. I *am* saying that *all* writers have their particular obsessions. Some are boozers, some dopers, some much-married and some frustratedly celibate. They are all a little crazy because you have to be crazy to try to make your living as a writer. There is nothing secure about the profession; even if you are blessed with a best-seller, the public's tastes can change and the income can suddenly disappear. I have known a few writers who made more than a million dollars on a book, and thousands who have never sold a word. Yet the craft of writing is hugely attractive to many people, and I have been asked for advice, probed for information, invited to dinner, offered money for reading manuscripts, plied for a connection to an agent or editor, and generally ravaged by the public's eager thirst for the inside track on how to get to be a writer. There isn't, of course, any school or established process through which one magically "graduates" as a writer. I always tell people that they won't do it if they can possibly avoid it because it's the hardest thing in the world to do, and since most of them have already got jobs and careers that provide a living, they're never going to be desperate enough to write down the things that are closest to their hearts, the things they know best, as all good writing does. The writer pays the highest price for extracting his little dollop of poetry out of the ravages of his experience.

I sat around nights in the course of all the moving and divorcing and writing this book and — undoubtedly to avoid writing — fantasized in my mind a complete academic course that would teach people everything about the Business of Literature. Lit Biz 101, it would be called. My idea was to save the time it took to answer everybody's queries by just telling them to take the course. That would separate the casual people and the ones who just wanted to get you to read their poems from the people who really wanted the technical information and were willing to pay for it. The idea carried me away so completely that I did in fact organize the course, and it was so in demand that we had to limit the classes to twenty students and turn prospective students away.

Lit Biz 101 was taught by a faculty of eight teachers over seven weekly meetings with coffee and brandy and Black Russians; it went on in the darkened offices of *The Weekly* or in the Miller & Mungo bookstore downstairs, in the funky downtown waterfront district. Bums and drunks were everywhere when class got out at 10 P.M. and we had to operate an escort service for those of the women students who were afraid to walk back to their cars alone. The worst a bum would do is ask you for a quarter, but they were middle-aged wives and mothers from the suburbs who didn't know Seattle bums. I taught the first session as an "introduction to the Biz of Lit. Nonfiction writing for a market. Literary agents and pursuit of contracts. Writing for periodicals. Anything else that comes to mind." The second week's class was led by Alan Furst, a novelist from Bainbridge Island, Washington, and

New York City, who regaled the students with tales
from the fiction business: "Writing for a market if you
can find it. Hopelessness, apathy, despair, copyrights."
After the two writers, easily the "crazy" part of the
course, the students got Bob Kaplan, a lawyer, and
George Bennett, an accountant, both of whom repre-
sent writers in the area and who talked about income
taxes, income averaging, deductions, estimated payments, state and local taxes, contracts, royalties, libel,
the writer and the law. The third session was always
intense, as people who had never published a word had
all sorts of complicated questions about their imagined
royalties. There was always one person in the class
who voiced the paranoia that some unscrupulous
editor or agent in New York could *steal* their idea or
their manuscript, since manuscripts can't (or couldn't
before the 1976 copyright law) be copyrighted until
they're published.

The fourth session was taught by David Brewster,
editor of *The Weekly*, and the course description he
wrote was rather more sober than the classes themselves: "The nature of magazine writing and how it
differs from other forms of journalism. A brief survey
of some developments in the genre . . . . The local
market for placing magazine articles, along with my
assessment of the kinds of articles these magazines are
interested in receiving . . . . Tactics for knocking over
editors. In short, how (and whether) to be a freelance
magazine writer." He was followed in the fifth week
by Dan Levant, editor and owner of Madrona Publishers, who did "The business of book publishing. What a

publisher does. The publishing decision. Editing and copy editing. Design and production. Advertising and promotion. Sales and distribution. Kinds of publishers. Big publishers and small. Small presses. Self publishing. Vanity presses." So far our students had had an opportunity to get drunk with the writers, figure out the taxes with the money men, and press their manuscripts on the editors. We concluded the course in the sixth and seventh weeks with classes led by a publisher's representative — or "salesman," frankly — and a retail bookseller. Gordon White, the rep, did a "publisher to market" lecture about bookstores, book clubs, the field, discount structures, returns, basic community liaisons between publishers and their market. He was a great hit with the students, who appreciated his direct and savvy knowledge about what's out there on bookstore shelves, and what sells. The final session was led by Peter Miller, my partner at Montana Books, who did "Operating a retail bookstore — all aspects from building, construction, buying, credit . . . . Bookstore mechanics, statistics, what to look for and what to hope for and what you will get, near precisely." To acquaint the class with the unique procedure of returning mass-market paperbacks, in which you rip off the cover and throw the *book* away since the postage rates make returning the book unprofitable and then send the covers on to the publisher for credit, Peter forced the students to rip off the covers of some of the most attractive and popular titles of the day — and wouldn't allow them to keep the beheaded leftover books. They had to mournfully discard *Zen and the Art of Motorcycle Maintenance* or *Even Cowgirls Get the Blues* if they expected to become booksellers, he said.

Now the students paid $80 each for all of this priceless education, and most of them reported that it was a bargain. We did the course with capacity enrollment several times over and each teacher got about $150 to $200 for his lecture — terrible pay on the national lecture circuit, but not bad for a local Seattle seminar of modest enrollment. We realized we could go on offering Lit Biz 101 forever and probably not run out of interested students. Our only overhead was the liquor costs, as the rent was free and we never bothered to incorporate. We even began to joke about expanding the concept to Lit Biz 102, wherein a maximum of five students work with one instructor on a specific project, such as producing a book or an issue of a magazine; Lit Biz 201, one student works with one instructor; Lit Biz 301, you fuck your instructor; Lit Biz 401, you're too fucked up to fuck your instructor. All of which reminds me to be embarrassed that our faculty was all male; if the same course were offered in New York, where there are many women editors, the faculty might be weighted in the opposite direction. Women certainly constituted a majority of our students.

We stopped giving the class, though, because like everything else it got boring after a number of times around, and it got more complicated the more thousands of dollars we handled. The bank and the lawyer both thought it had to be incorporated (nonprofit, educational), and that meant more paperwork, a bank account, a bookkeeper, etc. We chose instead to look for sponsors among existing universities and arts foundations — to make Lit Biz 101 a course offering in a regular academic catalogue. That'd be the end of the Black Russians in the classroom, we figured, but we'd be relieved of the tedious work of administering the thing. I am proud to say that of the eighty or so students we graduated (with a parchment diploma), none of them has written a book, to my knowledge. That means we did our job well. They learned enough about the writing of books in seven weeks to realize that it is an activity and occupation best left to those tormented introverts to whom it offers some relief from dreadful inner tensions.

The public's taste is unpredictable and times range from relative affluence to absolute poverty; it's a feast-or-famine trip. When my first couple of books succeeded, I had considerably more money than a young man without responsibilities knows what to do with; for a time in the early seventies, I used to travel around with a briefcase full of hundred-dollar bills, which I handed out to friends and strangers in need from Vermont to British Columbia. I'm reminded of a story Ephraim Doner told me of what happened to Henry Miller when, after years of poverty, he got his first $25,000 check from a publisher. Miller was, according to Doner, too intimidated by the check to go to the bank alone, and really wanted only to get $55 in cash on the check so he could pay a personal debt. Doner and Miller went to the bank together; Miller got his $55 and walked out of the bank, Doner said, "like a little child full of delight at getting an unexpected treat. He didn't *believe* the bank was going to give him $55 in cash on a deposit of $25,000. He was shaking like a leaf." Miller then spent the rest of the money liberally, giving much of it away to friends in need. Kurt Vonnegut got suddenly rich in 1970 when all of his novels were both republished and sold to the movies, and he adopted an expansive lifestyle in New York City after many modest years in Barnstable, Massachusetts. Tom Robbins went from being an art critic for the Seattle *P-I* newspaper to a best-selling novelist and object of much worship from young girls, to end up tormented in Seattle back-room bar nights over the fact that the I.R.S. was trying to take it all away from him. (I told him to get more dependents and start nonprofit foundations — in other words, give the money away in a fashion that would legally prevent Uncle Sam from getting it.) ('Cause no matter how you figure it, if you have more money than you need, you'll have to give some of it away, either to real people or to the government. The rich are notoriously good at juggling the figures so they wind up paying a much smaller percentage of tax on their income than, say, my parents do from their jobs.) My parents, in their hardworking way, understand that a writer's income is in the nature of a windfall or sweepstakes win and therefore almost more trouble than it's worth; they are firm believers in the value of the "regular paycheck," even if 30 percent is eroded in taxes. If I brought home a $20,000 royalty check, my mother would say I'd spend it up and be broke again and she wished I had a regular paycheck. And she's right, of course; I spend it and I'm broke again, even starving again — living on love, chicanery, and gall.

It's more than most people could stand. I remember when I had to turn over Xerox copies of my last three years' I.R.S. returns to the dentist from whom we bought our first house; he just wanted some evidence of my income. The first two years' returns were respectably in the $20,000 per annum range but the third one, reflecting our first year in Seattle and the big Crash of seventy-three, showed I had a taxable income after deductions of only $3,500. It was impossible for a family of four to live on $3,500, and I knew the dentist's confidence in us as buyers would be crushed by that I.R.S. return. So I added a one before the 3,500, making it $13,500, and Xeroxed it, then Xeroxed the Xerox copy, and so forth, until it was quite hazy, but legible. I knew I could pay the dentist his $150 a month, because if you can't pay $150 rent a month in this country you can't survive at all; the dentist got his money and cashed out of the house when we sold it, and nobody was hurt by my little white $10,000 lie. I'm telling you about it when I never told my wife (for fear it'd make her nervous or guilty), so you can see the kinds of little hells you have to go through in this profession.

I started writing when I was a small child — a family newspaper turned out on a kid's typewriter, letter by letter, in which I'd take up my concerns about what my sister or brothers were doing. I wrote through grammar school, great tomes, and all through high school and college, working for and editing the school newspapers. I also devoured books from the age of four or five, and habitually read a half-dozen books a week by the time I entered high school. In college years, I apprenticed in the summers with daily newspapers in Massachusetts, writing obituaries and police stories and covering city council meetings. I figured that by the time I was twenty-one and left college to start a news service in Washington, D.C., I had already written four or five thousand published news stories. I never wanted anything more than to be a writer, never toyed with being a fireman or a doctor or a cop, would have loved to become a baseball player but realized at the age of eight that I wouldn't make it when I hit a home run and literally *ran home.* I never imagined I could do anything else but write, and at times I imagined that I couldn't even do that anymore. I've never succeeded in holding a job.

My first book was an outgrowth of the many articles L.N.S. published about the antiwar movement and sundry other movements of the day. I was asked to write it by a sympathetic editor who actually traveled to our hardship settlement in Vermont and suffered the rigors of our outhouse to stand by my side and extract the last few pages. I wrote the second book, about communes, stark naked at the typewriter in our living room filled with people, dogs, cats, and others. The third and fourth books were more or less written on the run, all over America, Europe, Asia, and the fifth was written in Seattle in my kids' playroom with my four-year-old daughter in my lap and my year-old son crawling around exploring. In this, the sixth, I have discovered for the first time the conventional American nine-to-five schedule, extraordinary in my case only in that, during writing periods, I don't allow myself weekends or holidays of any sort.

For this book, I entered into a contract that paid an advance on royalties of $20,000, half on signing and the other half on delivery; of this sum, an agent and photographer were paid, and of course travel expenses added up to a few thousand more. It took two years to write the book, so it comes down to payment of about $7,500 a year to me. Still a miracle considering that I did not, of course, actually write the book every day for two years but worked at it intermittently with magazine and newspaper articles, children, bookstores, divorce, bankruptcy, romance, alcohol, and baseball all racing around in my brain at once. My stomach got the message and started to issue vicious pains, like a knife in the gut, which I could relieve only by going out in my backyard at night and screaming my mantra into the fishpond. (I had a different mantra every month; "I'm mad as hell and I'm not going to take it anymore!" or "I forgive all.") I get a royalty of 10 to 15 percent of the retail price of each hardcover copy sold, and half of any royalties from a paperback edition, the other half accruing to the cloth publisher. It's a decent and fairly typical book contract. In the event of a paperback, with the royalty being split in half, the writer is frequently earning 5 percent or less; so when you buy a three-dollar paperback, you've contributed about fifteen cents to the author. The original publisher, of course, takes the risk and makes the investment of the author's advance and the high initial production costs, so it is usually only through subsidiary rights (like paperbacks) that a book climbs out of the red. It may be an adventuresome life, but for most writers it doesn't lead to easy wealth or glory beyond our tolerances.

Whatever else happens, I'm usually grateful that most of my books are in print, that I can write some magazine pieces every year, teach the occasional class, cop a grant, that I can actually survive and contribute to the support of my kids in this fashion without holding a regular job. And the kids also provide me with a foundation of emotional support, a new generation to believe in and all that corny stuff that parents think about their kids. We naturally want the best possible world for them, now that we've gone and brought them into it. And I naturally want the greatest amount of time I can get to spend with them. They enjoy my time much more than my money, just as I do. They are like angels to me because they rescued me from a path of riotous youthful self-destruction and guided me onto one of relative enterprise and health, gave me hope for the future and joy in the present. They are my redemption.

Whatever I am worth in dollars and cents is worthless unless I am free. Freedom has been the word all along. We shouted for it in our youthful uprisings and yearn for it in our industrious middle years, but we have had to redefine it again and again. Our ancestors thought freedom was something you *fought for* with guns and ammunition — theirs was a very political freedom, freedom from taxes, oppression, starvation, and annihilation by tyranny or nature. It always required a struggle, a battle. Freedom was never freely given. It was a matter of wresting power from the hands of great, evil forces, of winning the power over your own life by fighting and dying, if necessary. This struggle is still going on in the world, and will probably never end. But it's a very limited application of the word.

We in the United States have already won most of those purely political freedoms, and yet we don't feel free. I am more than conscious of the discriminations against minority groups from women to homosexuals; it's been truly said that almost everybody belongs to a minority group now. And almost everybody feels some restraint on personal freedom of expression, even if it's only social disapproval and not legal repercussions. But we still live in one of the freest countries of the world, as even a token amount of travel abroad will prove.

At some point in recent history, the idea shifted from fighting to *paying for* freedom: that is, literally in monetary form. We somewhere got the notion that we could buy our freedom if we just had enough cash to quit working and start enjoying life. This is a dangerous and widespread mental aberration. The truth is that we have to work, and that we are happiest when our work is the great joy of our lives, not when we're loafing. We've denigrated the notion of work to our enormous loss. People are trying to buy freedom as slaves once bought it from their masters, but it's much too expensive, it's priceless, and they end up paying for it all their lives and never getting it.

So we've been led, as a nation, to explore inner freedom, to try to break the psychological bonds to our possessions which are the real cause of our enslavement. In the Hindu religion it's called *moksha*, complete lack of attachment to things of the world. (Which makes it O.K. to *have* them because, let's face it, most of us aren't willing to give them up.) The irony of our turning to Eastern religion for the inner freedom we seek is that the Japanese and Indians are giving us lessons in materialism at the same time. The Japanese can't stop themselves from producing like crazy, and the Indians are the most materialistic people in the world. Nobody appreciates and lusts after material things like a people who are starving and dying for lack of them. I gave an Indian peasant the shirt off my back; he held it up to the sun, stretched the fabric, examined every button and stitch, finally announced with toothless grin, "It's a good one. Made in U.S.A." Meantime people in Marin County or your town are paying $20 each for Indian shirts that are flimsy and insubstantial, but somehow holy in the current mode. Even our search for inner freedom costs money; the market for mantras is going steadily up while the Dow-Jones Index droops. A thousand false Christs pound the planet.

And there is still one definition to go. It is that freedom which allows you to have your kids and your possessions as long as you never think you own them, and which permits you to make a living independently doing what you enjoy doing, as long as you don't strive to make enough money to allow you to stop doing it. Nobody yet has earned such a great sum. If you can do what you like and actually enjoy your responsibilities, then you don't seek to escape them; they are not real chains but voluntary ties to your life's blood, your energy and identity. It's a neat trick, this cosmic profit, if you can manage it. You can own anything as long as it doesn't own you. It's all in your mind. But most people seem headed in the opposite direction as fast as they can go: there is real fear of a depression abroad in the land. People talk about it. Things seem so expensive. Corners must be cut. And we forget, if we think about it at all, that these economic flurries are as nothing compared to the grim want and poverty which prevails around the world. While we worry about the cost of a pound of coffee, two people for each of us are worrying about surviving another day.

You have to let go, to let it all go, before they'll let you have it. This is a contradiction in terms, which makes no sense until you feel it. Past the point of surrender lies the reward. I have already lived through the Great Depression and it was a killer but I'm still alive. All those hungry people out there are still alive and will cling to life by a thread or a hair if necessary, they never give up, they live in the face of doom — as do we. We make war, nuclear waste, and imagine that we can cheat and fool our fellows without suffering the natural justice of karma. We fancy that this is the single life we lead, that we must gain and get while we have a chance. Chained to our things as we are, we are miserable. Numbers are infinite, and even a long succession of them leaves more to be desired. We naturally want to live for some purpose higher than life itself.

Because life itself is still cheap. We live in, and reproduce, terribly vulnerable and mortal temples. But our happiness, peace and freedom, the things that matter to us while we're alive, are elusive feelings that blow in and out in the winds of our minds. Cosmic, or real, profit is thus something highly unreal, intangible, imaginary. And it's not for sale. In God We Trust.